LOVE THE

Leftovers

make two meals from one

MURDOCH BOOKS

Contents

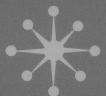

If you've been looking for ways to save precious time in the kitchen but still have everyone think you're the ultimate household hero, this book is for you. Here's the idea. You cook up a storm one day and make enough to provide the basis for two dinners or lunches. And the best part is: the extras you cook up the first day become a completely different, effortlessly conjured dish the next. We're not talking tired old leftovers here. Pork schnitzels with warm roasted beetroot and potato salad one night becomes the base for delicious beetroot ravioli with toasted walnuts the next, while extra tandoori roast chicken morphs seamlessly into chicken biryani, and artichoke and lemon veal chops stretch out to star in creamy veal and artichoke penne. Every delicious recipe has been specially devised to work to this cunning, time-saving concept, and the winner is you — twice over.

06 *Summer*

Summer calls for breezy flavours and quicker cooking styles. When the weather is warm and the living is easy you'll love the way steamed salmon with ginger rice transforms into salmon fried rice the next day. Or how leftover chickpea burgers become scrumptious fatoush, and extras from chicken with tuna mayonnaise and parmesan toasts converts into chicken caesar salad. Be clever, without cutting corners, and spend more time in the sun.

88 *Winter*

Hearty braises and nourishing soups bubbling on the stovetop, crusty oven roasts, lush casseroles, creamy mash, rich polenta and meaty pasta sauces are exactly what we crave when the air turns crisp. These sorts of dishes are all perfect for cooking in larger amounts, then putting to fresh use the next day. Cook double, save time and lose nothing in flavour with these deliciously heart-warming, soul-nourishing dishes.

Summer

Chickpea burgers • Spaghetti with leek, orange, basil and sun-dried tomatoes • Cuban picadillo • Steamed salmon with ginger rice • Stuffed Japanese beef rolls • Tex-Mex chicken and beans • Marinated steak stir-fry • Ricotta gnocchi with tomato, basil and cinnamon sauce • White-cooked chicken with ginger sauce • Cumin and cinnamon-dusted steak • Thai vegetable red curry • Honey-lime pork with ginger sweet potato mash • Steamed chicken with tuna mayonnaise and parmesan toasts • Chinese duck pancakes with five-spice and hoisin • Baked artichoke and lemon veal chops • Chargrilled chorizo and vegetables with romesco sauce • Pepperoni, capsicum and rocket braise with polenta • Chargrilled lamb cutlets with ratatouille and pesto • Singapore chicken curry with pineapple and cucumber salsa • Pork schnitzels with warm roasted beetroot and potato salad • Jerk chicken • Moroccan lamb skewers with couscous and chargrilled zucchini • Poached salmon with potatoes, broad beans and lemon and caper mayonnaise • Braised pork neck chops with star anise and orange • Coconut-poached chicken with noodles, bok choy and cashews • Roast lamb rump with fennel and celeriac remoulade • Baked snapper with lime-chilli dressing • Pork and Chinese sausage stir-fry • Roasted river trout • Poached lamb shanks with lemon and mint • Pork pot roast with tomato and lemongrass sauce • Japanese pork stir-fry • Lamb and pine nut rissoles • Chinese-style turkey stir-fry • Steak with spiced braised carrots • Teriyaki chicken with rice and vegetables • Curried lamb skewers with rocket, tomato and coriander salad • Chicken with tomato, fennel and lemon • Italian pork sausages with currant anchovy relish and roast vegetables • Tofu skewers with peanut sauce

Fattoush salad
Serves 4

Preheat the oven to 190°C (375°F/Gas 5). Cut the reserved pitta breads into small triangles, place on a baking tray and brush with olive oil. Bake for 10 minutes, or until golden and crisp. Remove from the oven and set aside. Meanwhile, place 2 small handfuls mint, 2 handfuls coriander (cilantro) leaves and 100 g (3½ oz) mixed baby salad leaves in a large salad bowl. Add 1 diced Lebanese (short) cucumber, 250 g (9 oz) halved cherry tomatoes, 1 small sliced red onion and 150 g (5½ oz/1 cup) pitted kalamata olives and toss gently. Crumble the reserved, room-temperature chickpea patties into the salad, then add the crisp pitta bread triangles. In a small bowl, whisk together 2½ tablespoons lemon juice, 2 teaspoons sumac, 2 crushed garlic cloves and 125 ml (4 fl oz/½ cup) extra virgin olive oil. Season to taste with sea salt and freshly ground black pepper, pour over the salad and toss to combine. Serve immediately.

Chickpea burgers

80 ml (2½ fl oz/⅓ cup) olive oil
6 x 15 cm (6 inch) wholemeal (whole-wheat) pitta breads
2 tomatoes, sliced
1 avocado, sliced
1 baby cos (romaine) lettuce, leaves washed and dried
Greek yoghurt, to serve
mint leaves, to serve

Chickpea patties

2 large desiree potatoes, about 550 g (1 lb 4 oz) in total, peeled and chopped into 3 cm (1¼ inch) chunks
2 x 400 g (14 oz) tins chickpeas, rinsed and drained
1 tablespoon tahini
4 garlic cloves, finely chopped
6 spring onions (scallions), thinly sliced
1 long red chilli, finely chopped
1 carrot, grated
1 teaspoon ground cumin
1 teaspoon ground coriander

To make the chickpea patties, cook the potatoes in a saucepan of boiling salted water for 20–25 minutes, or until tender. Drain and allow to cool, then mash and set aside.

Place the chickpeas in a food processor and blend until roughly chopped. Transfer to a large bowl and add the mashed potato, tahini, garlic, spring onion, chilli, carrot, cumin and coriander. Season with sea salt and freshly ground black pepper and mix well. Divide the mixture into 12 even portions, then shape into patties.

Heat half the olive oil in a large heavy-based frying pan over medium heat. Add half the patties and cook for 3 minutes each side, or until golden, taking care as you turn them as the patties are quite fragile. Remove and drain on kitchen paper, then repeat with the remaining oil and patties.

For the next day, reserve 2 pitta breads and 4 cooked patties for the fattoush salad. (The patties can be refrigerated in an airtight container for up to 3 days, but are not suitable for freezing.)

To assemble the burgers, cut the remaining pitta breads horizontally to open them up slightly. Divide the remaining patties, the tomato, avocado and lettuce among the pitta breads. Spoon in some yoghurt, top with mint leaves and serve.

Preparation time: 20 minutes   **Cooking time:** 40 minutes   **Serves:** 4

Preparation time: 10 minutes　　**Cooking time:** 15 minutes　　**Serves:** 4

Spaghetti with leek, orange, basil and sun-dried tomatoes

500 g (1 lb 2 oz) spaghetti
30 g (1 oz) unsalted butter
4 leeks, white part only, rinsed well
  and thinly sliced
2 garlic cloves, crushed
300 ml (10½ fl oz) cream
2½ teaspoons finely grated orange rind
80 ml (2½ fl oz/⅓ cup) orange juice
1 small handful basil, chopped
80 g (2¾ oz/½ cup) thinly sliced
  semi-dried (sun-blushed) tomatoes
50 g (1¾ oz/½ cup) shaved parmesan

Add the spaghetti to a large pot of rapidly boiling salted water and cook according to the packet instructions until al dente, about 10 minutes. Drain well.

Meanwhile, melt the butter in a large frying pan. Add the leek, season with sea salt and freshly ground black pepper and sauté over medium–low heat for 5 minutes, or until softened and light golden.

Add the garlic and cook for 2 minutes, then add the cream, orange rind and orange juice and simmer for 3–5 minutes.

Add the drained pasta, basil and sun-dried tomatoes, then toss well to coat the pasta with the sauce.

For the next day, reserve about 350 g (12 oz/2 cups) of the pasta mixture for the frittata, ensuring you have an even amount of all the ingredients. (The pasta mixture can be refrigerated in an airtight container for up to 3 days, but is not suitable for freezing.)

Divide the remaining pasta among serving bowls, scatter with the parmesan and serve.

Baked tuna, spinach and pasta frittata
Serves 4

Preheat the oven to 180°C (350°F/ Gas 4). In a large bowl, whisk 6 eggs and 100 ml (3½ fl oz) cream until combined. Stir in 50 g (1¾ oz/½ cup) grated parmesan, 2 tablespoons chopped basil, a drained 185 g (6½ oz) tin of flaked tuna and 100 g (3½ oz) baby English spinach leaves and season to taste with sea salt and freshly ground black pepper. Evenly spread the reserved pasta over the bottom of a greased 20 cm (8 inch) cake tin. Pour the egg mixture over and bake for 30 minutes, or until the frittata is lightly browned and the eggs are set. Allow to cool slightly, then cut into quarters. Serve with a green salad.

Cuban picadillo

Beef and avocado tacos
Serves 4 (makes 12)

Preheat the oven to 180°C (350°F/Gas 4). Reheat the reserved picadillo mixture in a saucepan; if necessary, boil the mixture until all excess liquid has evaporated (the mixture should be quite dry, or the tacos will be soggy). Place 12 taco shells in a large baking dish, then spoon the picadillo mixture into the shells. Sprinkle with 200 g (7 oz/1⅔ cups) grated cheddar cheese and bake for 15 minutes, or until the cheese has melted and the taco shells are heated through. Divide 1 diced avocado among the tacos, then top with a spoonful of sour cream and some coriander (cilantro) sprigs. Serve immediately.

1.25 kg (2 lb 12 oz) beef stewing steak, such as chuck, trimmed and cut into 4 cm (1½ inch) chunks
500 ml (17 fl oz/2 cups) beef stock
80 ml (2½ fl oz/⅓ cup) olive oil
2 onions, chopped
4 garlic cloves, chopped
2 large red capsicums (peppers), finely diced
2 teaspoons cumin seeds
½ teaspoon chilli flakes, or to taste
1½ tablespoons tomato paste (concentrated purée)
2½ teaspoons dried oregano
175 g (6 oz/1 cup) pimento-stuffed green olives, chopped
155 g (5½ oz/1¼ cups) raisins
1 kg (2 lb 4 oz) roma (plum) tomatoes, cut into 1 cm (½ inch) pieces
2½ tablespoons red wine vinegar
1 large handful coriander (cilantro), chopped
steamed rice, to serve
green salad, to serve

Place the beef in a large saucepan. Pour in the stock and enough cold water to just cover the beef. Bring slowly to a simmer, skimming off any froth that rises to the surface, then cook over low heat for 1 hour 40 minutes, or until the beef is very tender. Drain well, reserving the liquid for another use. Allow the meat to cool, then cut into 1 cm (½ inch) pieces and set aside.

Heat the olive oil in a large saucepan over medium heat. Add the onion and garlic and sauté for 4 minutes, or until beginning to soften. Add the capsicum and cook for 2 minutes, or until beginning to soften, then add the spices, tomato paste and oregano and cook for another 3 minutes, or until the mixture is fragrant and the vegetables are soft.

Add the olives, raisins, tomatoes, vinegar and chopped beef and stir until well combined. Cook for 4–5 minutes, or until the meat is heated through.

For the next day, reserve about 4 cups of the picadillo mixture for the tacos. (The picadillo mixture can be refrigerated in an airtight container for up to 3 days, or frozen for up to 2 months.)

Season the remaining picadillo mixture to taste with sea salt and freshly ground black pepper. Stir in the coriander and serve with steamed rice and a green salad.

Preparation time: 40 minutes   **Cooking time:** 2 hours   **Serves:** 4

✳ Preparation time: 15 minutes   **✳ Cooking time:** 30 minutes   **✳ Serves:** 4

Steamed salmon with ginger rice

2 tablespoons soy sauce
1 tablespoon rice vinegar
1 tablespoon shaved palm sugar
  (jaggery)
6 x 180 g (6 oz) skinless salmon fillets,
  pin bones removed
1 tablespoon sesame oil
6 baby bok choy (pak choy), halved
1 handful coriander (cilantro) leaves

Ginger rice
2 teaspoons sesame oil
1 onion, finely diced
1½ tablespoons finely chopped
  fresh ginger
1 garlic clove, crushed
400 g (14 oz/2 cups) jasmine rice

To make the ginger rice, heat the sesame oil in a saucepan over medium heat. Add the onion and sauté for 5 minutes, or until softened. Add the ginger and garlic and sauté for 2–3 minutes, or until fragrant, then add the rice and stir until coated in the oil. Pour in 670 ml (23 fl oz/ 2⅔ cups) water. Reduce the heat to low, then cover and cook for 12 minutes, or until the water has been absorbed and the rice is tender.

Meanwhile, half-fill a wok with water and place over medium heat. Sit a large steamer basket inside the wok, ensuring the water does not seep into the basket.

In a small bowl, whisk together the soy sauce, vinegar and palm sugar until the sugar has dissolved. Place the salmon fillets on a large plate inside the steamer and drizzle the soy mixture over each fillet. Steam for 6 minutes, or until the salmon is cooked to your liking.

While the salmon is steaming, heat the sesame oil in a large saucepan over medium–high heat. Add the bok choy, then cover and cook for 3–4 minutes, or until tender, shaking the pan often.

For the next day, reserve 2 salmon fillets, 4 bok choy halves and half the ginger rice for the salmon fried rice. (The ingredients can be refrigerated in airtight containers for up to 2 days, but are not suitable for freezing.)

Divide the remaining rice among four plates or wide shallow bowls. Top each with a salmon fillet and drizzle with any remaining soy sauce mixture. Sprinkle with the coriander and serve with the remaining bok choy.

Salmon fried rice
Serves 4

Flake the reserved salmon fillets into large chunks; cut the reserved bok choy into 2 cm (¾ inch) lengths. Heat 1 tablespoon peanut oil in a wok until smoking. Pour in 2 lightly beaten eggs and swirl the wok until the egg covers the base. Cook for 1–2 minutes, or until the egg has set. Tip the omelette onto a chopping board, roll it into a cylinder and thinly slice. Add the reserved ginger rice, bok choy and 200 g (7 oz/1 cup) tinned corn kernels to the wok and stir-fry for 5–6 minutes, or until the rice is starting to brown. Stir in the egg strips, flaked salmon, 90 g (3¼ oz/1 cup) bean sprouts, 2 tablespoons soy sauce and 1 handful coriander (cilantro) leaves and cook for a further 1 minute. Serve hot, with kecap manis or soy sauce on the side.

Stuffed Japanese beef rolls

Kushi-age
Serves 4 (makes 18)

Cut each reserved beef roll into three even slices on a slight diagonal. Place 2 tablespoons plain (all-purpose) flour in a bowl and season with sea salt and freshly ground black pepper. Whisk 1 extra large egg (or 2 small eggs) in another bowl, and spread 50 g (1¾ oz/1 cup) panko (Japanese breadcrumbs) on a plate. Roll each beef piece in the flour, then dip in the egg and evenly coat in the breadcrumbs. Heat about 5 cm (2 inches) of vegetable oil in a deep-fryer or large heavy-based saucepan to 180°C (350°F), or until a cube of bread dropped into the oil browns in 15 seconds. Cook the rolls in batches for 1–2 minutes, or until golden and tender, then drain on kitchen paper. Meanwhile, in a bowl, toss together 2 peeled and thinly sliced Lebanese (short) cucumbers, 2 tablespoons rice vinegar, 2 teaspoons caster (superfine) sugar and a pinch of salt. Just before serving, sprinkle with ½ tablespoon toasted sesame seeds and 2 tablespoons shredded nori. Serve with the hot beef rolls.

900 g (2 lb) beef eye fillet, trimmed, then cut into 18 thin slices
8 spring onions (scallions), cut into 10 cm (4 inch) lengths, plus extra spring onion slivers, to garnish
2 tablespoons vegetable oil
steamed white rice, to serve

Tamari ginger sauce
60 ml (2 fl oz/¼ cup) tamari or dark soy sauce
60 ml (2 fl oz/¼ cup) mirin
1 tablespoon soft brown sugar
1 tablespoon finely grated fresh ginger
¼ teaspoon sesame oil

Preheat the oven to 180°C (350°F/Gas 4).

Put the tamari ginger sauce ingredients in a small saucepan with 60 ml (2 fl oz/¼ cup) water and stir until the sugar has dissolved. Bring to the boil, then simmer gently over medium heat for 5–10 minutes, or until the mixture has reduced slightly and thickened. Set aside.

Working with one piece at a time, place the beef slices between two sheets of plastic wrap and pound with a meat mallet until about 10 x 15 cm (4 x 6 inches) in size.

Place a piece of spring onion along the short side of one slice of beef, then roll the beef tightly around the spring onion to form a log. Set aside and repeat with the remaining beef slices and spring onion pieces.

Heat a chargrill pan over high heat. Brush the beef rolls lightly with the oil. Working in batches, sear the rolls for 2–3 minutes, or until just golden, turning to brown on all sides.

Arrange the beef rolls in a 30 x 20 cm (12 x 10 inch) ceramic baking dish. Spoon the tamari ginger sauce over the rolls, making sure they are all well coated. Bake, uncovered, for 5–7 minutes, or until the beef is medium–rare.

For the next day, reserve 6 beef rolls for the kushi-age. (The rolls can be refrigerated in an airtight container for up to 2 days, but are not suitable for freezing.)

Divide the remaining beef rolls among serving plates, allowing three rolls per person. Drizzle with the tamari ginger sauce, garnish with spring onion slivers and serve with steamed white rice.

Preparation time: 30 minutes   **Cooking time:** 30 minutes   **Serves:** 4

Preparation time: 20 minutes   **Cooking time:** 1 hour   **Serves:** 4

Tex-Mex chicken and beans

60 ml (2 fl oz/¼ cup) olive oil

1 kg (2 lb 4 oz) minced (ground) chicken

2 large onions, finely chopped

3 garlic cloves, finely chopped

2 teaspoons ground cumin

1 tablespoon tomato paste
(concentrated purée)

2 x 400 g (14 oz) tins chopped tomatoes

250 ml (9 fl oz/1 cup) chicken stock

2 tablespoons soft brown sugar

1 long red chilli, finely chopped

½ teaspoon cayenne pepper, or to taste

2 x 400 g (14 oz) tins red kidney beans,
rinsed and drained

4 iceberg lettuce leaf cups (the inner
leaves are best)

lime halves, to serve

2 tablespoons chopped pickled jalapeño
chillies, to serve

grated mild cheddar cheese, to serve

crusty bread, steamed rice or warmed
flour tortillas, to serve

Salsa crudo

2 large tomatoes, finely chopped

1 onion, finely chopped

2 spring onions (scallions), sliced

2½ tablespoons chopped coriander
(cilantro) leaves

1 tablespoon lime juice, or to taste

Heat 2 tablespoons of the olive oil in a large heavy-based saucepan over medium heat. Add half the chicken and cook for 5 minutes, or until golden brown, breaking up any lumps with a wooden spoon. Transfer to a large bowl. Repeat with the remaining chicken, adding a little more oil if necessary. Set aside.

Heat the remaining oil in the same saucepan. Add the onion and sauté for 5 minutes, or until softened. Return the chicken to the pan, add the garlic, cumin and tomato paste and cook, stirring, for 1 minute. Stir in the tomatoes, stock, sugar, chilli and cayenne pepper. Bring to the boil, then cover, reduce the heat to low and simmer for 40 minutes. Stir in the beans and cook for 5 minutes to heat through.

Meanwhile, put all the salsa crudo ingredients in a bowl and toss until well combined. Season to taste with sea salt.

For the next day, reserve half the salsa crudo and one-third of the chicken mixture for the enchiladas. (The salsa crudo can be refrigerated in an airtight container for up to 2 days; the chicken mixture can be refrigerated in an airtight container for 4–5 days, or frozen for up to 2 months.)

Arrange the lettuce cups on serving plates and spoon the remaining salsa crudo into the leaves. Serve the remaining chicken mixture in warmed bowls, with lime halves, jalapeño chillies, grated cheese, and crusty bread, steamed rice or warmed flour tortillas.

Enchiladas
Makes 6

Preheat the oven to 180°C (350°F/Gas 4). Divide the reserved chicken mixture among 6 large soft tortillas and roll each one up. Place side by side in an oiled baking dish, seam side down. Spread the tops with sour cream and sprinkle with 125 g (4½ oz/1 cup) grated cheddar cheese. Cover loosely with foil and bake for 20 minutes. Remove the foil and bake for a further 10 minutes, or until the enchiladas are golden brown. Serve with the reserved salsa crudo and extra chopped pickled jalapeño chillies.

Green papaya and beef salad

Serves 4

Grate 500 g (1 lb 2 oz) peeled and seeded green papaya into a large bowl. Add 1 small thinly sliced red onion, 2 seeded, thinly sliced Lebanese (short) cucumbers, 2 tablespoons fish sauce, 2 tablespoons lime juice, 50 g (1¾ oz/⅓ cup) toasted chopped peanuts and the reserved beef. Toss gently to combine. Serve sprinkled with 1 small handful coriander (cilantro) leaves and 1 thinly sliced red chilli.

Marinated steak stir-fry

800 g (1 lb 12 oz) beef eye fillet or minute steak, thinly sliced
60 ml (2 fl oz/¼ cup) peanut oil
1 large red onion, thinly sliced
1 teaspoon finely grated fresh ginger
175 g (6 oz/1 bunch) broccolini, trimmed and thinly sliced on the diagonal
1 yellow capsicum (pepper), thinly sliced
1 tablespoon fish sauce
1 long red chilli, cut into long, thin strips
steamed jasmine rice, to serve
lime wedges, to serve

Soy and lime marinade
3 tablespoons chopped coriander (cilantro) stems and roots
1 garlic clove, crushed
2 tablespoons shaved palm sugar (jaggery)
2 tablespoons oyster sauce
2 tablespoons light soy sauce
2 tablespoons lime juice

Place the soy and lime marinade ingredients in a large bowl and mix until the sugar has dissolved. Add the beef slices and toss to coat well. Cover and marinate in the refrigerator for 3 hours.

Drain the beef well, reserving the marinade. Place a wok over high heat. Add half the peanut oil and cook the beef in batches for 2 minutes, or until browned, tossing regularly. Remove from the wok and set aside.

For the next day, reserve half the beef for the green papaya and beef salad. (The beef can be refrigerated in an airtight container for up to 2 days, but is not suitable for freezing.)

Heat the remaining oil in the wok. Add the onion, ginger, broccolini and capsicum and stir-fry for 2–3 minutes, or until the vegetables are just tender. Add the remaining beef slices, reserved marinade and fish sauce and toss until heated through.

Divide among serving bowls and garnish with the chilli strips. Serve with steamed jasmine rice and lime wedges.

Preparation time: 20 minutes
plus 3 hours marinating

Cooking time: 15 minutes

Serves: 4

Preparation time: 45 minutes Cooking time: 45 minutes Serves: 4

Ricotta gnocchi with tomato, basil and cinnamon sauce

750 g (1 lb 10 oz) firm fresh ricotta
225 g (8 oz/1½ cups) plain (all-purpose)
   flour, sifted, plus extra, for dusting
3 eggs
1 teaspoon freshly grated nutmeg
shredded or grated parmesan, to serve

Tomato, basil and cinnamon sauce
80 ml (2½ fl oz/⅓ cup) extra virgin
   olive oil
3 onions, finely chopped
3 garlic cloves, finely chopped
2 tablespoons tomato paste
   (concentrated purée)
330 ml (11¼ fl oz/1⅓ cups) red wine
5 x 400 g (14 oz) tins chopped tomatoes
3 teaspoons caster (superfine) sugar
1½ tablespoons balsamic vinegar
1½ cinnamon sticks
1 small handful basil leaves, torn

To make the tomato, basil and cinnamon sauce, heat the olive oil in a large saucepan over medium heat. Add the onion and garlic and sauté for 8 minutes, or until the onion is soft. Add the tomato paste and cook, stirring, for 2 minutes, then add the wine and boil for 2–3 minutes, or until slightly reduced. Stir in the tomatoes, sugar, vinegar and cinnamon sticks. Bring the mixture to a simmer, then reduce the heat to low and cook for 25 minutes. Discard the cinnamon sticks and season to taste with sea salt and freshly ground black pepper. Just before serving, stir in the basil.

Meanwhile, combine the ricotta in a large bowl with the flour, eggs and nutmeg. Season to taste, then mix together well.

Dust a work surface with flour. Divide the ricotta mixture into six portions. Using your hands, roll each portion into a rope about 2 cm (¾ inch) thick, then cut each one into 3 cm (1¼ inch) lengths.

Bring a large saucepan of salted water to the boil. Add the gnocchi in batches and cook for 3–4 minutes, or until they rise to the surface and are cooked through. Remove using a slotted spoon and keep warm.

For the next day, reserve 1 litre (35 fl oz/ 4 cups) of the tomato, basil and cinnamon sauce for the roast pumpkin and mozzarella lasagne. (The sauce can be refrigerated in an airtight container for up to 2 days, but is not suitable for freezing.)

Divide the gnocchi among serving bowls, then spoon the remaining sauce over. Scatter with parmesan and serve.

Roast pumpkin and mozzarella lasagne
Serves 4–6

Preheat the oven to 180°C (350°F/ Gas 4). Peel 1 kg (2 lb 4 oz) pumpkin (winter squash) and cut into slices 1 cm (½ inch) thick. Overlap them in a large oiled roasting tin, drizzle with olive oil and bake for 20 minutes, or until tender. Grease a 30 x 20 cm (12 x 8 inch) baking dish, then spread one-quarter of the reserved tomato sauce over the base. Place a single layer of instant lasagne sheets (from a 250 g/9 oz box) over the sauce. Spread half the pumpkin over in a single layer and spread with another one-quarter of the sauce. (You can also add thin slices of salami or prosciutto if desired.) Grate 225 g (8 oz) mozzarella cheese and scatter one-third over the sauce. Add another layer of lasagne sheets, then the remaining pumpkin, another one-quarter of the sauce and another one-third of the mozzarella. Top with a final layer of lasagne sheets, spread the remaining tomato sauce over and sprinkle with the remaining mozzarella. Cover with oiled foil and bake for 30 minutes. Remove the foil and bake for another 20 minutes, or until the cheese is golden and bubbling.

White-cooked chicken with ginger sauce

Bang bang chicken
Serves 4

Cook 200 g (7 oz) fresh Chinese wheat noodles in boiling water until tender, according to the packet instructions. Drain well, refresh under cold running water and drain again. Remove the meat from the reserved chicken, then shred. Place in a large bowl with the noodles, 2 seeded, thinly sliced Lebanese (short) cucumbers, 2 thinly sliced spring onions (scallions), 1 thinly sliced long red chilli and 1 small handful coriander (cilantro) leaves. Combine the reserved ginger sauce with 60 g (2¼ oz/½ cup) Chinese sesame paste (available from Asian food stores), 2 tablespoons hoisin sauce and 2 tablespoons hot water. Divide the chicken salad among serving bowls and drizzle with the sesame dressing. Sprinkle with toasted sesame seeds and serve.

1 litre (35 fl oz/4 cups) chicken stock
500 ml (17 fl oz/2 cups) dry sherry
6 garlic cloves, quartered
150 g (5½ oz) piece of fresh ginger, thinly sliced
2 tablespoons sea salt
2 teaspoons sesame oil
2 x 1.6 kg (3 lb 8 oz) whole chickens
300 g (10½ oz/1½ cups) long-grain white rice
2 spring onions (scallions), thinly sliced on the diagonal
1 small handful coriander (cilantro) leaves

Ginger sauce
125 ml (4 fl oz/½ cup) soy sauce
1 tablespoon rice vinegar
1½ tablespoons caster (superfine) sugar
1 tablespoon finely grated fresh ginger
2 teaspoons sesame oil

In a large saucepan, combine the stock, sherry, garlic, ginger, sea salt, sesame oil and 2 litres (70 fl oz/8 cups) water. Bring to the boil, then reduce the heat to low and simmer, uncovered, for 10 minutes.

Add the chickens to the stock mixture, adding extra water to just cover the chickens if necessary. Cook over low heat for 25 minutes. Without lifting the lid, remove the saucepan from the heat and allow to stand for 3 hours, or until the chickens are cooked through. Drain the chickens well, reserving the stock.

Combine the rice and 625 ml (21½ fl oz/ 2½ cups) of the reserved stock in a saucepan and bring to a simmer. Cover tightly, reduce the heat to low, then cook for 15 minutes, or until the rice is tender and the liquid has been absorbed. Allow to stand for 5 minutes.

Meanwhile, combine all the ginger sauce ingredients in a small bowl. Add 60 ml (2 fl oz/ ¼ cup) of the reserved chicken stock and stir until the sugar has dissolved.

For the next day, reserve 1 chicken and half the ginger sauce for the bang bang chicken. (The ingredients can be refrigerated in airtight containers for up to 2 days, but are not suitable for freezing.)

Using a cleaver or sharp knife, cut the remaining chicken into 4 or 8 pieces and divide among serving plates. Sprinkle with the spring onion and coriander, drizzle with the remaining ginger sauce and serve with the rice.

Preparation time: 30 minutes
plus 3 hours standing

Cooking time: 55 minutes

Serves: 4

Cumin and cinnamon-dusted steak

6 x 150 g (5½ oz) sirloin or rump
  steaks, each about 2 cm (¾ inch)
  thick
2 tablespoons olive oil, plus extra,
  for brushing
½ teaspoon ground cinnamon
1 teaspoon ground cumin
¼ teaspoon sweet paprika
1 teaspoon sea salt
2 onions, thinly sliced
2 red capsicums (peppers), thinly sliced
1–2 red chillies, finely chopped
1 garlic clove, finely chopped
1 tablespoon small oregano leaves
baked potatoes, to serve
sour cream, to serve
dijon mustard, to serve

Brush both sides of each steak with olive oil. In a small bowl, mix together the spices and sea salt and dust evenly over each side of each steak. Cover and set aside for 15 minutes.

Heat the olive oil in a heavy-based frying pan over medium heat. Add the onion and sauté for 5 minutes, or until softened. Add the capsicum, chilli, garlic and oregano and cook for 5–8 minutes, or until the capsicum is well softened, stirring occasionally.

Meanwhile, heat a chargrill pan or barbecue hotplate to high. Brush the steaks all over with more olive oil, then cook for 3 minutes on each side for medium, or until done to your liking. Remove to a warmed plate, cover loosely with foil and leave to rest for 5 minutes.

For the next day, reserve 2 steaks and half the capsicum mixture for the fajitas. (The ingredients can be refrigerated in airtight containers for up to 3 days, but are not suitable for freezing.)

Divide the remaining steaks among serving plates and top with the capsicum mixture. Serve with baked potatoes topped with a dollop of sour cream, and some dijon mustard on the side.

Fajitas
Serves 4

Preheat the oven to 150°C (300°F/Gas 2). Thinly slice the reserved steaks. Spread 8 small flour tortillas thinly with bought Mexican salsa, then arrange the steak slices and the reserved capsicum mixture lengthways down the centre of each. Roll up each tortilla, wrap each one in foil, place on a baking tray and bake for 10–15 minutes, or until heated through. Meanwhile, in a bowl, gently toss together 2 finely diced tomatoes, 1 chopped Lebanese (short) cucumber, 1 chopped avocado, 1 handful coriander (cilantro) leaves and the juice of 1 lime; season with sea salt. (For added kick, mix in a finely diced jalepeño chilli.) Transfer the tortilla wraps to serving plates and serve with the avocado salsa.

For a simpler version, serve the warmed fajitas with shredded iceberg lettuce, finely diced tomato, chopped avocado and sour cream.

Vegetable pasties

Serves 4

Preheat the oven to 200°C (400°F/ Gas 6). Place the reserved vegetables in a bowl with 80 g (2¾ oz/½ cup) thawed frozen peas and mix well, draining off any excess liquid. Thaw 4 sheets frozen puff pastry; working with one sheet at a time, place an inverted 15 cm (6 inch) saucer or plate on each pastry sheet and use a sharp paring knife to cut out 4 large pastry circles. Place one-quarter of the vegetable mixture in the centre of each pastry circle, fold one side of the pastry over to meet the other, then press the edges to seal, crimping them together with a fork. Place on a baking tray and bake for 20 minutes, or until the pastry is golden brown and cooked through. Serve hot, with a sweet chilli dipping sauce.

Thai vegetable red curry

1 tablespoon Thai red curry paste
2 garlic cloves, chopped
2 red Asian shallots, chopped
1 x 270 ml (9½ fl oz) tin coconut cream
1 x 400 ml (14 fl oz) tin coconut milk
250 ml (9 fl oz/1 cup) vegetable stock
2 desiree potatoes, peeled and cut into
  2 cm (¾ inch) chunks
150 g (5½ oz) sweet potato, peeled
  and cut into 2 cm (¾ inch) chunks
400 g (14 oz) broccoli, cut into florets
1 red capsicum (pepper), cut into
  strips 1 cm (½ inch) wide
1 carrot, cut in half lengthways,
  then thinly sliced
6 small button mushrooms
1 tablespoon fish sauce
1 tablespoon lime juice
1 tablespoon shaved palm sugar
  (jaggery)
1 small handful coriander (cilantro)
  leaves, chopped
chopped toasted peanuts, to serve
steamed jasmine rice, to serve
lime halves, to serve

Place the curry paste, garlic and shallots in a food processor and blend until a smooth paste forms. Set aside.

Pour the coconut cream into a wok or large saucepan and bring to the boil over medium heat. Reduce the heat to low and simmer for 10 minutes, or until the oil starts to separate from the cream and the surface appears shiny. Add the curry paste mixture and cook, stirring, for 3 minutes, or until fragrant

Pour in the coconut milk and stock and bring to a simmer. Add the potato and sweet potato, then cover and cook over medium–low heat for 10 minutes. Add the broccoli, capsicum, carrot and mushrooms. Cover and cook for 5 minutes, or until the vegetables are tender, tossing the wok occasionally.

Stir in the fish sauce, lime juice, palm sugar and coriander and cook for a further 3 minutes.

For the next day, drain off about 2 cups of the curried vegetables for the vegetable pasties. (The vegetables can be refrigerated in an airtight container for up to 3 days, or can be frozen for up to 4 weeks.)

Sprinkle the remaining curry with chopped toasted peanuts. Serve with steamed jasmine rice and lime halves.

Preparation time: 20 minutes   **Cooking time:** 35 minutes   **Serves:** 4

Preparation time: 40 minutes
plus up to 4 hours marinating

Cooking time: 30 minutes

Serves: 4

Honey-lime pork with ginger sweet potato mash

16 thin pork loin steaks or pork schnitzels, about 1.25 kg (2 lb 12 oz) in total
25 g (1 oz) butter
80 ml (2½ fl oz/⅓ cup) peanut oil
1 tablespoon finely chopped fresh ginger
900 g (2 lb) sweet potatoes, peeled and cut into 2 cm (¾ inch) chunks
1½ tablespoons toasted sesame seeds (optional)
baby English spinach leaves, to serve

Honey-lime marinade
3 garlic cloves, crushed
60 ml (2 fl oz/¼ cup) honey
80 ml (2½ fl oz/⅓ cup) Thai sweet chilli sauce
125 ml (4 fl oz/½ cup) lime juice
60 ml (2 fl oz/¼ cup) fish sauce
1 tablespoon sesame oil

In a small bowl, whisk together the honey-lime marinade ingredients. Pour half the mixture into a large bowl, add half the pork steaks and toss to coat well. Cover and refrigerate for up to 4 hours.

For the next day, reserve the remaining pork steaks and the remaining honey-lime marinade for the Chinese cabbage, herb and pork salad. (The ingredients can be refrigerated in airtight containers for up to 3 days, but are not suitable for freezing.)

In a saucepan, heat the butter and 2 tablespoons of the peanut oil over medium–low heat. Add the ginger and sauté for 2–3 minutes, or until fragrant. Add the sweet potato, stir to coat in the butter mixture, then cover and cook over low heat for 20–25 minutes, or until the sweet potato is very soft, stirring occasionally. Using a potato masher, mash the sweet potato and season to taste with sea salt and freshly ground black pepper. Cover and keep warm.

Meanwhile, heat the remaining oil in a large frying pan over medium–high heat. Drain the marinated pork well, discarding the liquid. Fry the pork in batches for 2 minutes on each side, or until just cooked through.

Divide the sweet potato mash and pork among serving plates. Sprinkle with the sesame seeds, if using, and serve with baby English spinach leaves.

Chinese cabbage, herb and pork salad with honey-lime dressing
Serves 4

Brush the reserved pork steaks with a little peanut oil, then chargrill or barbecue over medium heat for 2 minutes on each side, or until cooked through. Allow to cool, then cut into thin strips and place in a bowl. Add ½ small Chinese cabbage, very thinly sliced, 1 handful coriander (cilantro) sprigs, 1 handful mint, 1 thinly sliced red onion, 1 thinly sliced small red capsicum (pepper) and 1 large carrot, cut into thin matchsticks. Add the reserved honey-lime marinade and toss to coat well. Season to taste with sea salt and freshly ground black pepper and divide among serving bowls. Sprinkle with chopped roasted cashews and serve immediately, with steamed rice.

Chicken caesar salad

Serves 4–6

Preheat the grill (broiler) to medium–high. Grill (broil) 6 rindless bacon slices until crisp; allow to cool, then tear into large pieces into a bowl. Thinly slice the reserved chicken breasts and add to the bacon, along with the roughly torn leaves of 2 cos (romaine) lettuces. Add the reserved toasts, broken into large pieces. Add a little hot water to the reserved tuna mayonnaise to thin it down to a light coating consistency, then add to the salad with roughly chopped anchovies to taste. Toss well, divide among serving bowls, scatter generously with shaved parmesan and serve immediately.

Steamed chicken with tuna mayonnaise and parmesan toasts

16 slices of day-old baguette or ciabatta, cut on the diagonal into long widths about 5 mm (¼ inch) thick
olive oil, for brushing
50 g (1¾ oz/½ cup) grated parmesan
8 small chicken breast fillets, about 230 g (8 oz) each
300 g (10½ oz) green beans, trimmed
250 g (9 oz) yellow grape tomatoes, halved lengthways
2 large handfuls rocket (arugula)

Tuna mayonniase

4 egg yolks
2½ tablespoons white wine vinegar
1½ tablespoons dijon mustard
400 ml (14 fl oz) light olive oil
1 x 185 g (6½ oz) tin tuna in oil, undrained, flaked into large chunks
6 anchovies, roughly chopped

To make the tuna mayonnaise, blend the egg yolks, vinegar and mustard in a food processor until well combined. With the motor running, add the olive oil in a slow, steady stream; process until thick and emulsified. Add the undrained tuna and anchovies and pulse to combine. Add just enough hot water (about 2 tablespoons) to thin the mayonnaise to a thick, creamy consistency. Season to taste with sea salt and freshly ground black pepper. Transfer to a small bowl and cover the surface directly with plastic wrap to stop a skin forming. Cover and refrigerate for up to 4 days.

Preheat the oven to 180°C (350°F/Gas 4). Place the bread slices on a baking tray and brush with olive oil. Turn them over, brush the other side and bake for 6 minutes, or until light golden.

For the next day, reserve 10 toasted bread slices for the caesar salad and store in an airtight container. Also reserve half the tuna mayonnaise.

Scatter the parmesan over the remaining toasted bread slices and bake for 8 minutes, or until deep golden and crisp. Allow to cool, then break into small pieces into a large bowl.

Increase the oven temperature to 200°C (400°F/Gas 6) and heat a large roasting tin in the oven. Working quickly, add the chicken to the hot tin with 250 ml (9 fl oz/1 cup) boiling water. Season well, cover tightly with foil and bake for 25–30 minutes, or until the chicken is just cooked in the middle — take care not to overcook the chicken or it will be dry.

Meanwhile, cook the beans in boiling salted water until just tender; drain well and cool to room temperature. Add to the broken parmesan toasts with the tomatoes and rocket; gently toss, then divide among serving plates.

For the next day, reserve 4 chicken breasts for the salad. (They can be refrigerated in an airtight container for up to 3 days.)

Cut the remaining chicken breasts into thirds and arrange over the salads. Drizzle with the remaining tuna mayonnaise and serve.

Preparation time: 40 minutes   **Cooking time:** 45 minutes   **Serves:** 4

Preparation time: 20 minutes
plus 20 minutes resting

Cooking time: 30 minutes

Serves: 4

Chinese duck pancakes with five-spice and hoisin

150 g (5½ oz/1 cup) plain
   (all-purpose) flour
2 tablespoons cornflour (cornstarch)
1 tablespoon sesame seeds
125 ml (4 fl oz/½ cup) milk
2 eggs
2 teaspoons sesame oil
1 Chinese barbecued duck
vegetable oil, for pan-frying
4 spring onions (scallions), cut into
   5 cm (2 inch) lengths
1 Lebanese (short) cucumber, seeded
   and cut into thin strips
125 ml (4 fl oz/½ cup) hoisin sauce

In a bowl, mix together the flour, cornflour, sesame seeds and a pinch of sea salt, then make a well in the centre. Whisk together the milk, eggs, sesame oil and 125 ml (4 fl oz/½ cup) water, then gradually whisk into the flour mixture until smooth. Cover with plastic wrap and allow to rest for 20 minutes.

Meanwhile, carve the breasts from the duck, then thinly slice and set aside.

For the next day, reserve the remaining duck for the won ton soup. (The duck can be refrigerated in an airtight container for up to 2 days, but is not suitable for freezing.)

Heat a non-stick frying pan over medium heat. Lightly brush with vegetable oil. Spoon 2 tablespoons of the batter into the pan and spread to make a thin pancake, about 15 cm (6 inches) across. Cook for 1 minute, then turn the pancake over and cook for a further 30 seconds. Remove to a plate and repeat with the remaining batter to make 20 pancakes, brushing the pan with more oil as needed.

Place 2 duck breast strips, 2 spring onion pieces and 2 cucumber strips on each pancake. Drizzle each with 1 teaspoon hoisin sauce and roll up. Serve immediately, with the remaining hoisin sauce.

Duck won ton soup
Serves 4

Remove the meat from the reserved duck, then shred and refrigerate until required. Place the duck carcass in a large saucepan with a 3 cm piece of fresh ginger, peeled and cut into thin strips. Add 500 ml (17 fl oz/2 cups) chicken stock and enough water to just cover the bones. Bring to the boil over medium heat, then reduce the heat and simmer for 30–40 minutes. Strain the stock into a clean saucepan and bring back to the boil. Add 24 frozen won tons, the finely shredded duck meat and 100 g (3½ oz) sliced shiitake mushrooms and simmer for 5 minutes. Add 2 quartered baby bok choy (pak choy) and 2 tablespoons soy sauce and simmer for 2 minutes. Spoon the soup into serving bowls and garnish with bean sprouts, chopped garlic chives and coriander (cilantro) leaves. Serve with hot chilli sauce on the side.

Creamy veal and artichoke penne

Serves 4

Add 400 g (14 oz) penne to a large pot of rapidly boiling salted water and cook according to the packet instructions until al dente. Meanwhile, finely chop the meat from the reserved veal chops and place in a large non-stick frying pan with the reserved sauce, 125 ml (4 fl oz/½ cup) cream and 80 g (2¾ oz/½ cup) frozen peas. Bring to the boil over medium heat, then reduce the heat and stir 50 g (1¾ oz/½ cup) grated parmesan through. Cook for 2 minutes, or until the cheese has melted. Drain the penne well, then mix the sauce through with 1 small handful roughly chopped flat-leaf (Italian) parsley. Season with sea salt and freshly ground black pepper and serve.

Baked artichoke and lemon veal chops

60 ml (2 fl oz/¼ cup) olive oil
6 veal chops, about 1.25 kg (2 lb 12 oz) in total
1 onion, finely diced
2 garlic cloves, crushed
1 celery stalk, finely diced
2 rindless bacon slices, about 115 g (4 oz) in total, finely chopped
2 tablespoons plain (all-purpose) flour
500 ml (17 fl oz/2 cups) chicken stock
280 g (10 oz) jar of artichoke hearts, drained and cut in half lengthways
2 teaspoons finely grated lemon rind
2½ tablespoons lemon juice
steamed green beans, to serve
1 small handful flat-leaf (Italian) parsley, chopped (optional)

Soft polenta

250 ml (9 fl oz/1 cup) milk
250 ml (9 fl oz/1 cup) chicken stock
150 g (5½ oz/1 cup) instant polenta
50 g (1¾ oz/½ cup) grated parmesan
60 ml (2 fl oz/¼ cup) cream

Preheat the oven to 180°C (350°F/Gas 4).

Heat 2 tablespoons of the olive oil in a large frying pan over medium heat. Cook the veal chops in batches for 1 minute on each side, or until golden. Transfer to a baking dish.

Reduce the heat to medium–low and heat the remaining olive oil in the frying pan. Add the onion and garlic and sauté for 1 minute, or until the onion starts to soften. Add the celery and bacon and cook for a further 2 minutes, or until the bacon is golden.

Sprinkle the flour over and cook, stirring constantly, for 30 seconds, or until combined. Gradually pour in the stock, stirring until well combined and smooth. Bring to a simmer, stirring constantly to prevent lumps forming, then cook for 2–3 minutes, or until the sauce has thickened. Stir in the artichokes, lemon rind and lemon juice.

Spoon the sauce over the veal chops and bake for 10 minutes, or until the veal is tender.

Meanwhile, make the soft polenta. Combine the milk and stock in a heavy-based saucepan and bring to the boil over medium heat. Whisk in the polenta until incorporated. Stirring constantly with a wooden spoon, simmer for 2–3 minutes, or until the polenta thickens. Stir the parmesan and cream through and season to taste with sea salt and freshly ground black pepper.

For the next day, reserve 2 veal chops and 500 ml (17 fl oz/2 cups) of the sauce for the creamy veal and artichoke penne. (The ingredients can be refrigerated in airtight containers for 2 days, but are not suitable for freezing.)

Serve the chops with the soft polenta and steamed beans, sprinkled with the parsley if desired.

Preparation time: 20 minutes   **Cooking time:** 30 minutes   **Serves:** 4

Preparation time: 15 minutes **Cooking time:** 45 minutes **Serves:** 4

Chargrilled chorizo and vegetables with romesco sauce

8 chorizo sausages, cut on the diagonal into slices 1 cm (½ inch) thick
1 small sweet potato, about 350 g (12 oz), peeled and sliced 1 cm (½ inch) thick
1 eggplant (aubergine), about 450 g (1 lb), thinly sliced
2 yellow capsicums (peppers), cut into 4 cm (1½ inch) chunks
3 zucchini (courgettes), sliced 1.5 cm (⅝ inch) thick
2 red onions, cut into thin wedges
2 tablespoons olive oil
flat-leaf (Italian) parsley sprigs, to garnish

Romesco sauce

2 red capsicums (peppers), quartered, seeds and membranes removed
4 garlic cloves, unpeeled
2 tomatoes
80 g (2¾ oz/½ cup) whole blanched almonds
¼ teaspoon Spanish smoked paprika
1 tablespoon red wine vinegar
60 ml (2 fl oz/¼ cup) extra virgin olive oil
a pinch of chilli flakes (optional)

Preheat the grill (broiler) to high. To make the romesco sauce, place the capsicum on a baking tray, skin side up, with the garlic and whole tomatoes. Grill (broil) for 15 minutes, or until the skins are blackened. Allow to cool, then peel and discard the skins from the capsicum, garlic and tomatoes. Remove the seeds from the tomatoes. Place the capsicum, garlic and tomatoes in a food processor with the remaining romesco sauce ingredients and blend until smooth. Season to taste with sea salt and freshly ground black pepper and set aside.

Preheat a chargrill pan or barbecue hotplate to medium. Toss the sausages and vegetables in the olive oil and season with sea salt and freshly ground black pepper. Cook the sausages and vegetables in batches for 3–5 minutes on each side, or until all the vegetables are tender and the sausages are cooked through.

For the next day, reserve 10 chorizo sausage slices, one-quarter of the chargrilled vegetables and half the romesco sauce for the muffaletta. (The ingredients can be refrigerated in airtight containers for 2 days, but are not suitable for freezing.)

Arrange or layer the remaining vegetables and chorizo sausages in a large bowl or on a platter. Drizzle with the remaining romesco sauce, garnish with parsley sprigs and serve.

Muffaletta
Serves 4

Cut a round hole in the top of a 20 cm (8 inch) round loaf of bread, leaving a 1 cm (½ inch) border all around the edge and bottom. Hollow out and reserve the filling for another use; also reserve the lid. Slice 2 baby bocconcini and 2 roma (plum) tomatoes, season with sea salt and freshly ground black pepper and set aside. Spread the hollowed-out loaf with some of the reserved romesco sauce, then layer with the reserved chargrilled vegetables, reserved chorizo and the bocconcini and tomato slices, drizzling with the remaining romesco sauce as you go. When the loaf is filled, replace the lid. Wrap the loaf tightly in plastic wrap and refrigerate overnight. Cut into wedges for a shared picnic lunch or light supper.

Rustic scrambled eggs with fried polenta

Serves 4

Cut the reserved polenta into slices 1 cm (½ inch) thick. Heat 2 tablespoons olive oil in a large frying pan over medium–high heat. Fry the polenta in batches for 2 minutes on each side, or until golden and heated through; keep warm. Meanwhile, in a large saucepan, simmer the reserved pepperoni braise over medium heat for 5 minutes, or until the excess liquid has evaporated. Break 8 eggs into the braise, reduce the heat to low, then cover tightly and cook for 4 minutes, or until the eggs have set. Serve with the hot fried polenta.

Pepperoni, capsicum and rocket braise with polenta

60 ml (2 fl oz/¼ cup) extra virgin olive oil
300 g (10½ oz) thin hot pepperoni salami, cut into slices 1 cm (½ inch) thick
2 red capsicums (peppers), cut into thin strips
1 yellow capsicum (pepper), cut into thin strips
3 onions, thinly sliced
2 garlic cloves, thinly sliced
400 g (14 oz) grape tomatoes, halved
250 ml (9 fl oz/1 cup) good chicken stock
2 small handfuls rocket (arugula), roughly chopped

Polenta
425 ml (15 fl oz) milk
300 ml (10½ fl oz) chicken stock
1½ teaspoons sea salt flakes
185 g (6½ oz/1¼ cups) polenta
50 g (1¾ oz/½ cup) grated parmesan

To make the polenta, combine the milk, stock, sea salt and 750 ml (26 fl oz/3 cups) water in a large saucepan and bring to the boil over medium heat. Whisking constantly, add the polenta in a slow steady stream. Reduce the heat to low and cook for 35 minutes, or until very thick, stirring often.

Meanwhile, heat the olive oil in a large frying pan over medium heat. Add the pepperoni, capsicum, onion, garlic and a pinch of sea salt. Reduce the heat to medium–low and cook for 10 minutes, or until the vegetables are softened but not coloured, stirring often. Add the tomatoes and stock and cook for a further 20 minutes.

For the next day, reserve 375 ml (13 fl oz/ 1½ cups) of the polenta and half the pepperoni braise for the scrambled eggs with fried polenta. Spread the polenta on a board to form a 10 x 15 cm (4 x 6 inch) rectangle, allow to cool, then wrap and refrigerate. (The ingredients can be refrigerated in airtight containers for 2 days, but are not suitable for freezing.)

Add the parmesan to the remaining polenta and stir well; the polenta will be a little sloppy. Stir the rocket through the remaining pepperoni braise.

Divide the polenta among wide shallow serving bowls, top with the pepperoni braise and serve.

Preparation time: 20 minutes   **Cooking time:** 40 minutes   **Serves:** 4

Preparation time: 20 minutes　　　Cooking time: 50 minutes　　　Serves: 4

Chargrilled lamb cutlets with ratatouille and pesto

1 eggplant (aubergine), cut into 3 cm (1¼ inch) chunks
1½ teaspoons dried oregano
60 ml (2 fl oz/¼ cup) olive oil, plus extra, for brushing
1 red onion, sliced
2 garlic cloves, crushed
2 zucchini (courgettes), cut into 1 cm (½ inch) rounds
1 red capsicum (pepper), cut into 3 cm (1¼ inch) chunks
400 g (14 oz) tin whole tomatoes
2 teaspoons finely chopped lemon thyme
1 dried bay leaf
12 French-trimmed lamb cutlets
crusty bread, to serve

Pesto

3 large handfuls basil leaves
1 garlic clove
40 g (1½ oz/¼ cup) pine nuts
50 g (1¾ oz/½ cup) grated parmesan
185 ml (6 fl oz/¾ cup) olive oil, plus extra, for covering the pesto

To make the pesto, place the basil, garlic, pine nuts and parmesan in a food processor and blend until finely chopped. With the motor running, gradually add the olive oil in a thin steady stream until smooth, then season to taste with sea salt and freshly ground black pepper. Transfer to a clean container and cover the surface of the pesto with a drizzle of olive oil to stop the pesto discolouring. Refrigerate until required; the pesto will keep for up to 3 days.

Preheat the oven to 200°C (400°F/Gas 6). Line a baking tray with baking paper.

Place the eggplant and oregano in a bowl. Drizzle with 2 tablespoons of the olive oil and toss to coat. Spread the eggplant on the baking tray in a single layer and bake for 20 minutes, or until golden. Remove from the oven and set aside.

Heat the remaining oil in a large heavy-based saucepan over medium heat. Add the onion and garlic and sauté for 3–4 minutes, or until the onion is starting to soften. Add the zucchini, capsicum, tomatoes, thyme, bay leaf, eggplant and 125 ml (4 fl oz/½ cup) water. Bring to the boil, then reduce the heat to medium–low, cover and simmer for 20 minutes, or until the vegetables are soft.

Meanwhile, heat a chargrill pan or barbecue hotplate to medium. Cook the lamb cutlets, in batches if necessary, for 3 minutes on each side, or until just cooked through.

For the next day, reserve 2 ladlefuls of the ratatouille for the baked eggs. (The ratatouille can be refrigerated in an airtight container for 2 days, but is not suitable for freezing.)

Divide the remaining ratatouille among serving plates, then top with the lamb cutlets and a dollop of pesto. Serve with crusty bread.

Baked eggs with ratatouille and parmesan
Serves 4

Preheat the oven to 200°C (400°F/Gas 6). Spoon the reserved ratatouille into four lightly oiled 250 ml (9 fl oz/1 cup) ramekins. Crack an egg into each one and sprinkle each with 1 tablespoon finely grated parmesan. Place the ramekins in a baking dish and pour enough boiling water into the dish to come halfway up the sides of the ramekins. Bake for 10–12 minutes, or until the egg whites are just set and the yolk is still soft. Serve with hot toast spread with leftover pesto for a great brunch, or with crisp salad leaves for a light lunch.

Spiced chicken soup with noodles

Serves 4

Place 250 g (9 oz) vermicelli rice noodles in a large heatproof bowl. Cover with boiling water and soak for 5 minutes, or until softened; drain and set aside. Place the reserved chicken curry in a large saucepan, then stir in 270 ml (9½ fl oz) light coconut milk, 500 ml (17 fl oz/2 cups) chicken stock and 1 tablespoon fish sauce. Bring to the boil over medium heat. Add 3–4 thinly sliced baby bok choy (pak choy) and cook for 1 minute, or until just wilted. Divide the noodles among serving bowls and ladle the soup over. Top with 90 g (3¼ oz/1 cup) trimmed bean sprouts, 1 small handful coriander (cilantro) leaves, 1 small handful mint and 1 seeded and thinly sliced long red chilli. Serve immediately.

Singapore chicken curry with pineapple and cucumber salsa

1½ tablespoons peanut oil
1 onion, thinly sliced
800 g (1 lb 12 oz) chicken thigh fillets, trimmed and cut into 4 cm (1½ inch) chunks
185 g (6½ oz) jar Malaysian curry paste
2 potatoes, peeled and cut into 2 cm (¾ inch) chunks
400 ml (14 fl oz) tin coconut milk
1 red capsicum (pepper), thinly sliced
steamed rice, to serve
coriander (cilantro) leaves, to serve

Pineapple and cucumber salsa

1 Lebanese (short) cucumber, seeded and chopped
125 g (4½ oz/1 cup) fresh pineapple chunks
1 long red chilli, seeded and cut into long strips
2 tablespoons rice vinegar
1 tablespoon shaved palm sugar (jaggery)
2 teaspoons fish sauce
1 teaspoon lemon juice

Heat half the peanut oil in a wok or large frying pan over high heat. Add the onion and sauté for 2 minutes, or until just softened. Remove the onion to a plate.

Heat the remaining oil in the wok. Add the chicken in batches and stir-fry for 5 minutes, or until golden. Remove to a plate.

Return the onion to the wok, add the curry paste and cook, stirring, for 1 minute, or until aromatic. Add the potatoes, chicken, coconut milk and 125 ml (4 fl oz/½ cup) water and bring to the boil. Reduce the heat to low, cover and simmer for 15 minutes, or until the potatoes and chicken are tender. Add the capsicum and cook for a further 2 minutes, or until just softened.

Meanwhile, put all the pineapple and cucumber salsa ingredients in a large ceramic or glass bowl with a pinch of salt. Stir to combine, then cover and set aside for 10 minutes to allow the flavours to develop.

For the next day, reserve about 2 cups of the chicken curry for the spiced chicken soup. (The chicken curry can be refrigerated in an airtight container for 2 days, but is not suitable for freezing.)

Serve the chicken curry with the pineapple and cucumber salsa and steamed rice, garnished with coriander leaves.

Preparation time: 15 minutes   **Cooking time:** 40 minutes   **Serves:** 4

Preparation time: 30 minutes   **Cooking time:** 1 hour 45 minutes   **Serves:** 4

Pork schnitzels with warm roasted beetroot and potato salad

500 g (1 lb 2 oz) pork fillet, trimmed and cut into 8 equal portions
115 g (4 oz/2 cups) panko (Japanese breadcrumbs)
2 teaspoons dried oregano
1 teaspoon dried mint
1 handful flat-leaf (Italian) parsley, chopped
2 teaspoons finely grated lemon rind
150 g (5½ oz/1 cup) plain (all-purpose) flour
2 eggs
2 tablespoons olive oil
lemon wedges, to serve

Roasted beetroot and potato salad
4 large beetroot (beets), trimmed
4 large desiree potatoes, peeled and cut into 2 cm (¾ inch) chunks
2 large handfuls baby rocket (arugula)
2 tablespoons balsamic vinegar
2 tablespoons extra virgin olive oil

Preheat the oven to 180°C (350°F/Gas 4). To make the roasted beetroot and potato salad, wrap each beetroot in foil, place on a baking tray and bake for 1 hour. Put the potatoes on the same baking tray and shake to distribute them evenly. Bake for another 30 minutes, or until the beetroot and potatoes are tender.

While the beetroot and potato are roasting, prepare the pork schnitzels. Place the pork fillets between two sheets of baking paper and gently flatten using a rolling pin or meat mallet. Combine the panko, oregano, mint, parsley and lemon rind in a shallow bowl. Place the flour in another shallow bowl. In a third shallow bowl, lightly beat the eggs. Dust the pork fillets with the flour, then dip into the egg, then the panko mixture. Place each piece on a plate and refrigerate until needed.

Remove the roasted beetroot and potato from the oven. Leave the beetroot until cool enough to handle, then, wearing gloves to keep your hands from staining, peel off and discard the skins.

For the next day, reserve 1 beetroot and 6 potato pieces for the beetroot ravioli. (The ingredients can be refrigerated in airtight containers for 2 days, but are not suitable for freezing.)

Heat the olive oil in a large non-stick frying pan over medium heat. Add the pork schnitzels and fry in batches for 2–3 minutes on each side, or until golden and cooked through. Drain on kitchen paper and keep warm.

Meanwhile, cut the remaining beetroot into wedges and gently toss in a bowl with the remaining potatoes, rocket, vinegar and extra virgin olive oil.

Divide the beetroot and potato salad among serving plates. Top with the pork schnitzels and serve with lemon wedges.

Beetroot ravioli with toasted walnuts
Serves 4

Grate the reserved beetroot and potato pieces into a large bowl. Melt 50 g (1¾ oz) butter in a large non-stick frying pan over medium–low heat. Add 1 finely diced onion and sauté for 3 minutes, or until soft. Add the beetroot and potato and cook for 3 minutes, or until heated through. Remove from the heat and stir 250 g (9 oz) mascarpone and 75 g (2½ oz/¾ cup) grated parmesan through. Season to taste with sea salt and freshly ground black pepper and allow to cool. To make the ravioli, place a tablespoon of the mixture in the middle of 12 won ton or gow gee (egg) dumpling wrappers. Brush the edge with a little water, then top with another wrapper and seal. Place the ravioli in a single layer on trays lined with baking paper and set aside. Melt 100 g (3½ oz) butter in a small frying pan over medium heat. Add 60 g (2¼ oz/½ cup) chopped toasted walnuts and cook for 5 minutes, or until the butter is golden brown; remove from the heat and stir in 2 teaspoons lemon juice and 1 small handful flat-leaf (Italian) parsley. Add the ravioli to a large saucepan of salted boiling water and cook for 2 minutes; drain. Divide among shallow serving bowls, spoon the walnut butter over and serve.

Chicken, pineapple and avocado salad

Serves 4

Remove the meat from the reserved chicken pieces, discarding the bones. Thickly shred the chicken meat and place in a large bowl with the reserved pineapple and sweet potato. Add 100 g (3½ oz) mixed salad leaves, 1 small handful coriander (cilantro) leaves and ½ small, thinly sliced red onion. Drizzle with 1 tablespoon extra virgin olive oil, season with sea salt and freshly ground black pepper and gently toss. Thickly slice 1 avocado and drizzle with the juice of 1 lime; arrange over the salad and serve.

Jerk chicken

2 x 1.2 kg (2 lb 10 oz) chickens, each cut into 8 pieces
1 large sweet potato, about 600 g (1 lb 5 oz), peeled and cut into 2 cm (¾ inch) chunks
1 ripe pineapple, cut into 4 cm (1½ inch) chunks
2 tablespoons olive oil
60 ml (2 fl oz/¼ cup) lime juice
1 small handful coriander (cilantro) leaves
100 g (3½ oz) mixed salad leaves

Thyme and chilli marinade
2 onions, roughly chopped
3 long red chillies, roughly chopped
150 ml (5 fl oz) white wine vinegar
150 ml (5 fl oz) dark soy sauce
2 tablespoons finely chopped fresh ginger
20 g (¾ oz/1 bunch) thyme, leaves picked
1½ teaspoons ground allspice

Combine all the thyme and chilli marinade ingredients in a food processor and blend until a paste forms. Transfer to a large bowl, add all the chicken pieces and toss to coat, rubbing the marinade in well. Cover and marinate in the refrigerator for 8 hours, or overnight.

Preheat the oven to 180°C (350°F/Gas 4).

In a large bowl, toss the sweet potato and pineapple with the olive oil and lime juice, then spread in a roasting tin. Place the undrained chicken pieces in another roasting tin, then transfer both tins to the oven and roast for 35 minutes, or until the chicken is cooked through and the sweet potato is tender.

For the next day, reserve half the chicken pieces, half the pineapple and half the sweet potato for the salad. (The ingredients can be refrigerated in airtight containers for 2 days, but are not suitable for freezing.)

Toss the remaining pineapple and sweet potato in a bowl with the coriander and salad leaves. Divide among serving plates or shallow bowls. Top with the chicken pieces, drizzle with the juices from the roasting tin and serve.

Preparation time: 25 minutes
plus 30 minutes marinating

Cooking time: 15 minutes

Serves: 4

Moroccan lamb skewers with couscous and chargrilled zucchini

800 g (1 lb 12 oz) lamb backstraps
   or loin fillets, cut into 3 cm (1¼ inch)
   chunks
6 zucchini (courgettes), sliced lengthways
   about 3 mm (⅛ inch) thick
1 tablespoon extra virgin olive oil
375 ml (13 fl oz/1½ cups) chicken stock
40 g (1½ oz) butter
500 g (1 lb 2 oz/2¾ cups) instant
   couscous
1 teaspoon finely grated lemon rind
1½ tablespoons lemon juice
½ red onion, finely diced
1 large handful coriander (cilantro) leaves,
   plus extra, to garnish

Moroccan marinade
1 tablespoon Moroccan spice mix
   (available in supermarkets)
2 garlic cloves, crushed
1 teaspoon sea salt flakes
1 teaspoon finely grated lemon rind
1½ tablespoons lemon juice
1 tablespoon extra virgin olive oil

Soak 8 wooden skewers in cold water for 30 minutes to prevent scorching. Meanwhile, in a small bowl, mix together the Moroccan marinade ingredients. Place the lamb in a bowl, add the marinade and toss to coat, rubbing the mixture in well; cover and marinate in the refrigerator while the skewers soak.

In a bowl, toss the zucchini slices with the olive oil and season well with sea salt and freshly ground black pepper. Set aside.

In a saucepan, bring the stock and 375 ml (13 fl oz/1½ cups) water to the boil. Remove from the heat, add the butter and stir until melted. Place the couscous in a heatproof bowl, season well and pour the stock over. Mix well with a fork to separate the grains, then cover.

For the next day, reserve half the couscous for the couscous salad. (The couscous can be refrigerated in an airtight container for 2 days, but is not suitable for freezing.)

Add the lemon rind and lemon juice to the remaining couscous and mix again with a fork to separate the grains.

Meanwhile, heat a barbecue hotplate or chargrill pan to medium–high. Thread the lamb onto the soaked skewers and cook for 2 minutes on each side, or until done to your liking. Remove to a plate, cover and keep warm.

Increase the heat to high, then barbecue or chargrill the zucchini slices for 2 minutes on each side, or until just cooked. Remove the zucchini from the heat, roughly chop, then stir it through the couscous with the onion and coriander. Season to taste.

Spoon the couscous onto serving plates. Top with the lamb skewers, sprinkle with extra coriander and serve.

Warm couscous salad with apricots, feta and mint
Serves 4

Put the reserved couscous in a bowl and bring to room temperature. Drain and rinse a 400 g (14 oz) tin of chickpeas and add to the couscous. In a small saucepan, combine 375 ml (13 fl oz/1½ cups) orange juice, 1 small cinnamon stick, a pinch of chilli flakes, a large pinch of ground allspice and 1 teaspoon soft brown sugar and bring to a simmer. Cook for 5 minutes, or until reduced by half, then stir in 1 tablespoon olive oil and season to taste with sea salt and freshly ground black pepper. Add to the couscous with 150 g (5½ oz/1 cup) crumbled feta cheese, 75 g (2½ oz/⅓ cup) pitted green olives and 6–8 sliced fresh apricots (or drained, sliced tinned apricots). Add 1 handful torn mint leaves, ½ chopped long red chilli and 60 g (2¼ oz/⅔ cup) toasted flaked almonds. Toss well and serve.

Preheat the oven to 180°C (350°F/Gas 4). Spread 160 g (5½ oz/2 cups) fresh breadcrumbs on a baking tray and bake for 5 minutes, or until crisp but not coloured. Tip into a bowl. In another bowl season some plain (all-purpose) flour with sea salt and freshly ground black pepper. In a third bowl, beat 2 eggs. Mash the reserved potato mixture in a large bowl. Flake the reserved salmon and fold it through the potato mixture with 1½ tablespoons dijon mustard. Mix well, then shape into 8 patties, each about 7.5 cm (3 inches) in diameter. Lightly coat in the flour, then dip in the beaten eggs, then coat in the breadcrumbs. Heat 2 tablespoons vegetable oil in a large frying pan. Add the patties and cook over medium heat for 2–3 minutes on each side, or until golden and crisp. Serve with lemon cheeks, a green salad and the reserved lemon and caper mayonnaise.

Poached salmon with potatoes, broad beans and lemon and caper mayonnaise

1 tablespoon ground coriander
1 teaspoon sea salt
1½ teaspoons lemon thyme
finely grated rind of 2 lemons
80 ml (2½ fl oz/⅓ cup) olive oil
8 x 180 g (6 oz) skinless salmon fillets
8 medium zip-lock bags
1.5 kg (3 lb 5 oz) desiree potatoes, peeled and sliced 1 cm (½ inch) thick
2 onions, chopped
500 g (1 lb 2 oz/3¼ cups) frozen broad (fava) beans, thawed and peeled

Lemon and caper mayonnaise
170 ml (5½ fl oz/⅔ cup) whole-egg mayonnaise
1 tablespoon lemon juice
2 tablespoons drained capers, chopped

In a small bowl, mix together the ingredients for the lemon and caper mayonnaise. Cover and refrigerate until required.

Bring a large saucepan of water to a simmer, then remove from the heat and leave to stand for 5 minutes.

Meanwhile, put the coriander, sea salt, thyme and half the lemon rind and half the olive oil in a large bowl. Mix well, then add the salmon fillets and turn to coat both sides.

Place each salmon fillet in a zip-lock bag and seal. Gently place the bags in the saucepan of water, then return the saucepan to low heat and cook for 4 minutes, turning the bags over once. Remove the saucepan from the heat and allow to stand for 15 minutes. Remove the bags from the water.

Meanwhile, bring another large saucepan of salted water to the boil. Add the potato slices and simmer for 15 minutes, or until just tender. Drain and set aside.

Heat the remaining oil in a large frying pan over medium–low heat. Add the onion and a pinch of sea salt and sauté for 15 minutes. Add the broad beans and potatoes and gently heat through.

For the next day, reserve 4 salmon fillets for the salmon patties, leaving them in the bags. Also reserve half the potato mixure and half the lemon and caper mayonnaise in airtight containers. (The ingredients can be refrigerated for up to 2 days, but are not suitable for freezing.)

Tip the salmon cooking liquid from the remaining poaching bags over the remaining potato mixture and gently toss to combine. Divide among serving plates, top with the salmon fillets and serve with the remaining lemon and caper mayonnaise.

Preparation time: 20 minutes
plus 20 minutes standing

Cooking time: 40 minutes

Serves: 4

Braised pork neck chops with star anise and orange

6 dried shiitake mushrooms
60 ml (2 fl oz/¼ cup) olive oil
8 pork neck chops, each 2 cm (¾ inch) thick, about 1.25 kg (2 lb 12 oz) in total
8 French shallots, peeled
250 ml (9 fl oz/1 cup) white wine
750 ml (26 fl oz/3 cups) chicken stock
2 star anise
2 cinnamon sticks
2 wide orange zest strips
3 garlic cloves, sliced
80 ml (2½ fl oz/⅓ cup) orange juice

Ginger bok choy stir-fry

1 tablespoon peanut or vegetable oil
4 baby bok choy (pak choy), halved lengthways
1 garlic clove, thinly sliced
2 teaspoons finely chopped fresh ginger

Preheat the oven to 180°C (350°F/Gas 4). Soak the shiitake mushrooms in a bowl of warm water for 20 minutes, or until softened. Drain well, reserving the liquid. Remove and discard the mushroom stalks.

Heat the olive oil in a large heavy-based frying pan over medium heat. Cook the chops in batches for 2–3 minutes on each side, or until browned. Remove to a large roasting tin.

Add the shallots to the frying pan and sauté for 4 minutes, or until softened. Add the wine, bring to a simmer and cook for 5 minutes, or until the liquid has reduced by half. Add the mushrooms, reserved mushroom water and all but 60 ml (2 fl oz/¼ cup) of the stock. Add the star anise, cinnamon sticks, orange zest strips and garlic and mix well.

Pour the mixture over the chops. Cover tightly with foil and bake for 1½ hours, or until the pork is very tender.

For the next day, reserve 2 chops for the pork, pear and parsnip salad. (The chops can be refrigerated in an airtight container for up to 3 days, but are not suitable for freezing.)

Using tongs, remove the remaining chops, shallots and mushrooms to a warmed serving platter. Cover and keep warm.

Place the roasting tin over medium–high heat. Stir in the orange juice and bring to a simmer. Cook for 5–8 minutes, or until the liquid has reduced and thickened slightly. Strain into a serving jug and discard the solids.

To make the ginger bok choy stir-fry, heat the peanut oil in a large non-stick frying pan over medium–high heat. Add the bok choy, garlic and ginger and stir-fry for 1 minute. Add the reserved chicken stock and stir-fry for a further 30 seconds, or until the bok choy has just wilted.

Slice the pork into chunks. Serve with the vegetables and pan juices.

Pork, pear and parsnip salad
Serves 4

Preheat the oven to 190°C (375°F/Gas 5). Peel and quarter 2 firm pears and 4 small parsnips lengthways, removing the cores from the pears. Toss in a bowl with some olive oil, then spread in a small roasting tin. Season with sea salt and freshly ground black pepper and bake for 45 minutes, or until just cooked through. In a bowl, combine 1½ tablespoons sherry vinegar and 1 tablespoon extra virgin olive oil or 2 teaspoons nut oil (such as hazelnut). Add the hot parsnip and pear and toss to coat. Remove the meat from the reserved pork chops and slice finely; add to the bowl with a mix of chicory (witlof), snow pea (mangetout) sprouts and rocket (arugula) or watercress leaves. Toss gently and serve.

Pumpkin, coconut and chicken soup

Serves 4–6

Strain the reserved poaching broth, discarding the solids and any fat. Heat 2 tablespoons peanut oil in a large saucepan and sauté 2 chopped onions and 2 crushed garlic cloves for 5 minutes, or until softened. Add 1 kg (2 lb 4 oz) peeled, chopped butternut pumpkin (squash), then cover and cook for 25 minutes, or until the pumpkin is very soft, stirring occasionally. Add the poaching broth, bring to a simmer, then cover and cook for 5 minutes. Using a food processor or blender, process the mixture until smooth, then return to the saucepan. Strip the meat from the reserved chicken, discarding the bones, skin and fat. Shred or chop the meat finely, then add to the soup and bring to a simmer. Cook for 5 minutes, or until the chicken is heated through. Serve immediately, sprinkled with thinly sliced kaffir lime leaves and chopped coriander (cilantro).

Coconut-poached chicken with noodles, bok choy and cashews

2 x 1.2 kg (2 lb 10 oz) chickens
2½ tablespoons peanut oil
1 tablespoon finely chopped fresh ginger
1 bird's eye chilli, finely chopped, plus extra sliced red chilli, to serve
180 g (6 oz/2 cups) bean sprouts, tails trimmed
4 baby bok choy (pak choy), sliced
2 tablespoons soy sauce
400 g (14 oz) fresh rice noodles
50 g (1¾ oz/⅓ cup) roasted cashew nuts, chopped
coriander (cilantro) sprigs, to serve

Poaching broth
2 whole lemongrass stems, trimmed, bruised and each tied in a knot
100 ml (3½ fl oz) fish sauce
70 g (2½ oz/½ cup) grated palm sugar (jaggery)
5 cm (2 inch) piece of fresh ginger, peeled and thinly sliced
3 garlic cloves, bruised
5 kaffir lime leaves, bruised
400 ml (14 fl oz) tin coconut milk
750 ml (26 fl oz/3 cups) chicken stock, approximately

Rinse the chickens inside and out, then drain well. Place them sideways in a saucepan just large enough to fit them both snugly. Add the poaching broth ingredients and enough of the stock to just cover the chickens. Cover the pan tightly with a lid, then very slowly bring just to a simmer — try not to remove the lid, and do not allow the liquid to simmer fast or the chickens will toughen.

Slowly simmer the chickens for 1 hour, then remove the pan from the heat. Leave the lid on and leave to stand for 45 minutes. Remove the chickens from the poaching broth.

For the next day, reserve 1 chicken for the pumpkin, coconut and chicken soup. (The chicken and poaching broth can be refrigerated in airtight containers for up to 3 days, but are not suitable for freezing.)

Cut the remaining chicken into quarters, then return to the hot poaching broth to keep warm.

Heat the peanut oil in a wok over high heat. Add the ginger and chilli and fry for 1 minute, or until fragrant. Add the bean sprouts, bok choy and soy sauce and stir-fry for 3–4 minutes, or until the bok choy has just wilted.

Meanwhile, place the noodles in a heatproof bowl and cover with boiling water. Soak for 2 minutes, or until heated through. Drain well.

Gently toss the vegetables through the noodles and divide among shallow serving bowls. Place a chicken portion over each, reserving the poaching broth for the pumpkin, coconut and chicken soup.

Scatter with the cashews, coriander and extra chilli and serve.

Preparation time: 20 minutes
plus 45 minutes standing

Cooking time: 1 hour 15 minutes

Serves: 4

Preparation time: 20 minutes   Cooking time: 20 minutes   Serves: 4

Roast lamb rump with fennel and celeriac remoulade

500 g (1 lb 2 oz) trussed cherry
  tomatoes
1 tablespoon vegetable oil
4 x 250 g (9 oz) lamb rumps
  (mini roasts)
80 ml (2½ fl oz/⅓ cup) lemon juice
1 small celeriac, about 320 g (11¼ oz)
1 fennel bulb, about 450 g (1 lb),
  trimmed and thinly sliced widthways
185 g (6½ oz/¾ cup) whole-egg
  mayonnaise
2 teaspoons dijon mustard
2 tablespoons drained capers, finely
  chopped
2 tablespoons finely snipped chives

Preheat the oven to 200°C (400°F/Gas 6).
Line a baking tray with baking paper.

Cut the trussed tomatoes into 4 small
bunches. Place on the baking tray and set aside.

Heat the oil in a non-stick frying pan over
medium heat. Add the lamb rumps and cook for
2 minutes on each side, or until browned.

Transfer the lamb to the baking tray with the
tomatoes and roast for 15 minutes, or until done
to your liking. Remove the lamb to a plate, cover
loosely with foil and leave to rest for 5 minutes.

Meanwhile, add 2 tablespoons of the lemon
juice to a large bowl of water. Peel and grate the
celeriac, adding it to the water as you go to stop
it browning. Drain well, then toss the celeriac
in a large bowl with the fennel, mayonnaise,
remaining lemon juice, mustard, capers and
most of the chives.

For the next day, reserve 2 lamb rumps and
200 g (7 oz/1 cup) of the celeriac remoulade
for the lamb and remoulade sandwiches. (The
ingredients can be refrigerated in airtight
containers for up to 3 days, but are not suitable
for freezing.)

Divide the remaining remoulade among
serving plates. Carve the remaining lamb rumps
and arrange the slices over the remoulade.
Sprinkle with the remaining chives and serve
with the roasted tomatoes.

Lamb and remoulade sandwiches
Serves 4

Lightly toast 8 slices of sourdough
bread until golden. Spread each
slice with a little butter. Spoon the
reserved remoulade onto 4 slices
of toast. Slice the reserved lamb
rumps and place on top, along with
slices of tomato and some thinly
sliced red onion. Top with the
remaining toasts and serve.

Baked snapper with lime-chilli dressing

Snapper, cucumber and rice salad

Serves 4

In a large bowl, bring the reserved rice to room temperature. Remove the skin from the reserved snapper fillets, flake the fish and add to the rice. Add 2 small seeded and sliced cucumbers, 1 small finely chopped red onion, 90 g (3¼ oz/1 cup) trimmed bean sprouts, 1 handful mint and 1 handful coriander (cilantro) leaves and toss well. Mix together 60 ml (2 fl oz/¼ cup) lime juice, 1½ tablespoons fish sauce, 1 tablespoon shaved palm sugar (jaggery) and 1–2 seeded and finely chopped small red chillies. Drizzle the dressing over the salad and serve sprinkled with fried Asian shallots.

400 g (14 oz/2 cups) jasmine rice
8 x 150 g (5½ oz) snapper fillets, skin on, pin bones removed
2 cm (¾ inch) piece of fresh ginger, peeled and cut into thin matchsticks
1 garlic clove, thinly sliced
1 lime, thinly sliced
60 ml (2 fl oz/¼ cup) light soy sauce
2 tablespoons peanut oil
4 baby bok choy (pak choy), halved lengthways
3 spring onions (scallions), thinly shredded
1 small handful coriander (cilantro) leaves

Lime-chilli dressing
60 ml (2 fl oz/¼ cup) lime juice
2 tablespoons soft brown sugar
2 tablespoons fish sauce
1 long red chilli, seeded and finely chopped

Preheat the oven to 200°C (400°F/Gas 6).

Put the lime-chilli dressing ingredients in a small bowl. Stir until the sugar has dissolved, then set aside until required.

Put the rice in a saucepan with a pinch of sea salt. Pour in 625 ml (21½ fl oz/2½ cups) water. Bring to a simmer, then cover tightly and cook over low heat for 12 minutes. Leaving the lid on, remove the rice from the heat and leave to stand for 10 minutes.

Meanwhile, using a small knife, score three lines through the skin of each snapper fillet. Place the fillets in a large baking dish, skin side up, then arrange the ginger, garlic and lime slices over the top. Pour the soy sauce, peanut oil and 250 ml (9 fl oz/1 cup) boiling water over. Bake for 8–10 minutes, or until the fish is just cooked through.

While the fish is baking, cook the bok choy in a saucepan of salted boiling water for 2 minutes, or until tender.

For the next day, reserve 2 fish fillets and 375 g (13 oz/2 cups) of the steamed rice for the snapper, cucumber and rice salad. (The ingredients can be refrigerated in airtight containers for up to 2 days, but are not suitable for freezing.)

Divide the bok choy and remaining fish fillets among serving plates. Garnish with the spring onion and coriander, drizzle with the lime-chilli dressing and serve with the remaining rice.

✳ **Preparation time:** 15 minutes ✳ **Cooking time:** 15 minutes ✳ **Serves:** 4

Preparation time: 20 minutes
plus 2 hours marinating

Cooking time: 20 minutes

Serves: 4

Pork and Chinese sausage stir-fry

300 g (10½ oz) pork fillet, trimmed
  and thinly sliced
400 g (14 oz/2 cups) jasmine rice
1 tablespoon peanut oil
2 Chinese sausages (lap cheong),
  thinly sliced on the diagonal
200 g (7 oz/3⅓ cups) broccoli florets
1 red capsicum (pepper), sliced
4 spring onions (scallions), shredded,
  plus extra, to garnish
100 g (3½ oz) enoki mushrooms
  (optional)

Tamari garlic marinade
½ teaspoon bicarbonate of soda
  (baking soda)
1 teaspoon cornflour (cornstarch)
2½ tablespoons chicken stock
1½ tablespoons tamari
1 tablespoon Chinese chilli garlic sauce
1 tablespoon Chinese rice wine
2 teaspoons soft brown sugar
2 garlic cloves, crushed

Combine the tamari garlic marinade ingredients in a ceramic, glass or stainless steel bowl. Add the pork slices and toss until well coated. Cover and refrigerate for 2 hours.

Put the rice in a saucepan with a pinch of sea salt. Pour in 625 ml (21½ fl oz/2½ cups) water. Bring to a simmer, then cover tightly and cook over low heat for 12 minutes. Leaving the lid on, remove the rice from the heat and leave to stand for 10 minutes.

Meanwhile, drain the pork, reserving the marinade. Heat the peanut oil in a wok over high heat. Add the pork in two batches and stir-fry for 1–2 minutes, or until golden. Remove to a plate and keep warm.

Wipe the wok clean if necessary. Add the Chinese sausage and stir-fry for 2 minutes, or until golden. Add the broccoli and capsicum and stir-fry for 1 minute. Add 2 tablespoons water and cover with a lid to steam the vegetables for 1 minute. Add the spring onion and mushrooms, if using, and stir-fry for 1–2 minutes.

Pour in the reserved tamari garlic marinade and return the pork to the wok. Bring to a simmer and cook for 1–2 minutes to heat through.

For the next day, reserve 375 g (13 oz/2 cups) of the cooked rice for the Asian rice soup. (The rice can be refrigerated in an airtight container for up to 2 days, but is not suitable for freezing.)

Divide the remaining rice among four serving bowls. Top with the stir-fry mixture, garnish with extra shredded spring onion and serve.

Asian rice soup
Serves 4

Put the reserved rice in a large pot with 2 litres (70 fl oz/8 cups) chicken stock, 1 bruised lemongrass stem, 2 fresh ginger slices and 2 washed coriander (cilantro) stems and roots. Bring to the boil, reduce the heat to low, then cover and gently simmer for 15 minutes, stirring occasionally. Remove the coriander, lemongrass and ginger. Add 2 very thinly sliced baby bok choy (pak choy) and 2 tablespoons soy sauce and simmer for 1–2 minutes. Ladle into serving bowls, sprinkle with thinly sliced spring onion (scallion) and flavour with a few drops of sesame oil. You can also add some diced firm tofu, cooked shredded chicken or 12 peeled, deveined raw king prawns (shrimp) to the soup before serving, allowing 2–3 minutes for the ingredients to heat through and/or cook.

Roasted river trout

Roast cauliflower, trout and bean salad with tahini dressing
Serves 4

Bring the reserved trout, cauliflower and beans to room temperature. Remove and discard the skin and bones from the fish, then flake the flesh into a bowl. Add the cauliflower and beans and gently mix together. In a small bowl, combine 1 crushed garlic clove, 2 tablespoons Greek yoghurt, 1 tablespoon lemon juice, 1 tablespoon tahini and 1 tablespoon water and mix well. Drizzle over the salad, add 1 handful torn flat-leaf (Italian) parsley and toss. Sprinkle with sumac and serve.

6 x 350 g (12 oz) whole river trout
400 g (14 oz) tin chopped tomatoes
4 garlic cloves, crushed
1 teaspoon sweet paprika
1 tablespoon lemon juice
1 teaspoon caster (superfine) sugar
1 head of cauliflower, broken into florets
1 tablespoon ground cumin
35 g (1¼ oz/⅓ cup) flaked almonds
2½ tablespoons olive oil
350 g (12 oz) green beans, trimmed
1 small handful flat-leaf (Italian) parsley
lemon wedges, to serve

Preheat the oven to 200°C (400°F/Gas 6).

Place all the fish in a large baking dish, overlapping them slightly if necessary. In a small bowl, mix together the tomatoes, garlic, paprika, lemon juice and sugar, then pour over the fish. Cover with foil and bake for 30–35 minutes, or until the fish is just cooked through.

Meanwhile, bring a saucepan of water to the boil. Add the cauliflower and cook for 5 minutes, then remove using a slotted spoon and plunge into a bowl of iced water. Drain well, then dry completely with kitchen paper. Toss in a bowl with the cumin, flaked almonds and olive oil until coated. Transfer to a baking tray and bake for 10 minutes, or until golden.

While the cauliflower and fish are baking, bring the saucepan of water back to the boil and cook the beans for 3–4 minutes, or until tender.

When the trout are cooked, sprinkle with the parsley and season with sea salt and freshly ground black pepper.

For the next day, reserve 2 trout, half the cauliflower and half the beans for the roast cauliflower, trout and bean salad. (The ingredients can be refrigerated in airtight containers for up to 2 days, but are not suitable for freezing.)

Divide the remaining trout, cauliflower and beans among serving plates and serve with lemon wedges.

Preparation time: 20 minutes   Cooking time: 35 minutes   Serves: 4

✳ Preparation time: 30 minutes   **✳ Cooking time:** 2 hours 20 minutes   **✳ Serves:** 4

Poached lamb shanks with lemon and mint

2 tablespoons olive oil
8 French-trimmed lamb shanks
4 garlic cloves, peeled
750 ml (26 fl oz/3 cups) chicken stock
rind of 1 lemon, cut into 1 cm (½ inch) strips, white pith removed
2 bay leaves
400 g (14 oz) kipfler (fingerling) potatoes
1 small handful mint
1 small handful coriander (cilantro) leaves
2½ tablespoons lemon juice
Greek yoghurt, to serve

Tomato salsa
4 roma (plum) tomatoes, diced
1 tablespoon flat-leaf (Italian) parsley
1 tablespoon chopped mint
1 tablespoon extra virgin olive oil

Preheat the oven to 180°C (350°F/Gas 4).

Heat the olive oil in a large frying pan over medium–high heat. Add the shanks in batches and cook for 5 minutes, or until browned all over, turning often. Transfer to one large or two medium-sized roasting tins.

Add the garlic to the frying pan and sauté over medium heat for 2–3 minutes, or until softened. Pour in the stock and bring to the boil, stirring to remove any stuck-on bits from the bottom of the pan.

Pour the hot stock over the shanks. Season the shanks with sea salt and freshly ground black pepper and add the lemon rind strips and bay leaves. Cover with foil and bake for 1 hour.

Add the potatoes, then cover again and cook for another 1 hour, or until the shanks and potatoes are very tender.

Combine the mint, coriander and lemon juice in a small food processor. Blend until a paste forms, adding some cooking liquid from the lamb shanks to thin it if necessary. Stir the mixture through the lamb shanks and bake without the foil for a final 3 minutes. Adjust the seasoning.

In a bowl, toss together the tomato salsa ingredients and season with black pepper.

For the next day, reserve 4 shanks and 250 ml (9 fl oz/1 cup) of the cooking liquid from the shanks for the Middle-Eastern lamb salad. (The ingredients can be refrigerated in airtight containers for up to 4 days; the cooking liquid can be frozen for up to 2 months.)

Serve the remaining lamb shanks and potatoes in wide shallow bowls, with the tomato salsa and some yoghurt for spooning over.

Middle-Eastern lamb salad
Serves 4

Preheat the oven to 180°C (350°F/Gas 4). Place 2 small (or 1 large) pitta breads on a baking tray and bake for 5–10 minutes, or until golden and crisp. Meanwhile, remove the meat from the reserved lamb shanks, then shred and set aside. Drain and rinse a 400 g (14 oz) tin of chickpeas; place in a food processor with 1 large crushed garlic clove and the reserved lamb cooking liquid, then blend to a purée. Mix 1 crushed garlic clove through 250 g (9 oz/1 cup) Greek yoghurt; set aside. Break the pitta breads into bite-sized pieces and spread on serving plates. Drizzle with the chickpea purée, then the garlic yoghurt. Top with the shredded lamb and 1 handful mint leaves. Scatter 1 diced tomato over the top and serve.

Pork, tomato and lemongrass noodles with peanuts
Serves 6

Trim any fat and skin from the reserved pork, then finely chop the meat and place in a saucepan with the remaining tomato sauce mixture. Cover and slowly bring to a simmer; reduce the heat to very low and keep warm. Put 800 g (1 lb 12 oz) wide fresh rice noodles in a large heatproof bowl, cover with boiling water and soak for 3 minutes, or until soft. Drain the noodles well and divide among serving bowls. To the tomato sauce mixture add 1 handful torn Thai basil, 3 finely chopped spring onions (scallions) and a pinch of chilli flakes; stir well, then ladle over the noodles. Top with coriander (cilantro) sprigs and chopped roasted peanuts. Serve immediately.

Pork pot roast with tomato and lemongrass sauce

3 garlic cloves, chopped
2 tablespoons roughly chopped fresh ginger
4 lemongrass stems, white part only, roughly chopped
80 ml (2½ fl oz/⅓ cup) vegetable oil
2 onions, finely chopped
1 tablespoon tomato paste (concentrated purée)
2½ tablespoons caster (superfine) sugar
80 ml (2½ fl oz/⅓ cup) fish sauce
125 ml (4 fl oz/½ cup) chicken stock
2 x 800 g (1 lb 12 oz) tins chopped tomatoes
1.8 kg (4 lb) boned, rolled pork forequarter roast
green salad, to serve

Place the garlic, ginger and lemongrass in a food processor and blend until very finely chopped.

Heat half the oil in a large heavy-based saucepan or flameproof casserole dish. Add the onion and sauté over medium heat for 5–6 minutes, or until softened. Add the lemongrass mixture and cook, stirring, for 2–3 minutes, or until softened and fragrant. Stir in the tomato paste and cook for 1–2 minutes, then add the sugar, fish sauce, stock and tomatoes. Stir together well, then bring to a gentle simmer. Reduce the heat to very low, then cover and keep the sauce hot.

Meanwhile, heat the remaining oil in a large heavy-based frying pan. Add the pork roast and cook for 7–8 minutes, or until golden all over, turning often. Season the pork with sea salt and freshly ground black pepper.

Add the pork to the tomato sauce mixture. Partially cover the pan with a lid, then cook over very low heat for 2–2¼ hours, or until the pork is cooked through and very tender. Remove the pork from the sauce, cover with foil and keep warm.

Bring the tomato sauce mixture to a simmer and cook for 15 minutes, or until reduced by about one-third.

For the next day, reserve half the pork and most of the tomato sauce mixture for the pork, tomato and lemongrass noodles. (The ingredients can be refrigerated in airtight containers for up to 3 days, but are not suitable for freezing.)

Cut the remaining pork into 8 slices and divide among serving plates. Spoon the remaining tomato sauce over each. Serve with a green salad.

Preparation time: 35 minutes   **Cooking time:** 2 hours 40 minutes   **Serves:** 4

Preparation time: 10 minutes
plus 30 minutes marinating

Cooking time: 20 minutes

Serves: 4

Japanese pork stir-fry

80 ml (2½ fl oz/⅓ cup) soy sauce
1 tablespoon mirin
1 garlic clove, crushed
1 tablespoon finely grated fresh ginger
900 g (2 lb) pork fillets, thinly sliced
2½ tablespoons vegetable oil,
    approximately
1 onion, thinly sliced
200 g (7 oz) snow peas (mangetout),
    sliced in half on the diagonal
4 spring onions (scallions), cut into
    long strips
steamed rice, to serve

In a bowl, combine the soy sauce, mirin, garlic and ginger. Add the pork and toss to coat, then cover and marinate in the refrigerator for 30 minutes. Drain well, reserving the marinade.

Heat half the oil in a wok over high heat. Add the onion and sauté for 5 minutes, or until softened. Remove to a plate using a slotted spoon.

Heat another 1 tablespoon of oil in the wok. Stir-fry the pork in batches for 2–3 minutes, or until light golden, adding a little more oil as necessary, and removing each batch to a plate.

Add the reserved marinade to the wok and cook for 2 minutes, or until reduced by half. Return the pork and onion to the wok with the snow peas. Stir-fry for 1–2 minutes, or until the snow peas are just tender and the pork is heated through.

For the next day, reserve half the pork stir-fry for the okonomiyaki. (The mixture can be refrigerated in an airtight container for up to 2 days, but is not suitable for freezing.)

Divide the remaining pork stir-fry among serving bowls. Scatter with the spring onion and serve with steamed rice.

Pork okonomiyaki
Serves 4

In a large bowl, lightly whisk 4 eggs with 250 ml (9 fl oz/1 cup) chicken stock. Sift in 300 g (10½ oz/2 cups) self-raising flour, mix until well combined, then allow to rest for 20 minutes. Stir in 75 g (2½ oz/ 1 cup) thinly sliced Chinese cabbage and a pinch of sea salt. Heat 1 tablespoon vegetable oil in a non-stick frying pan, pour in one-quarter of the batter and cook for 4–5 minutes, or until golden. Top the pancake with one-quarter of the reserved pork stir-fry and 45 g (1½ oz/¼ cup) chopped firm tofu and cook for a further 2 minutes. Flip the pancake over and cook for 2 minutes, or until the pancake is set all over. Remove from the pan and keep warm. Repeat to make another 3 pancakes. Serve with Japanese barbecue sauce.

Lamb and pine nut rissoles

Turkish bread sandwiches with tabouleh

Serves 4

Place 45 g (1½ oz/¼ cup) fine burghul (bulgur) in a bowl and add 125 ml (4 fl oz/½ cup) boiling water. Cover and set aside. Roughly chop 150 g (5½ oz/1 bunch) flat-leaf (Italian) parsley and place in a bowl. Add 1 seeded, chopped Lebanese (short) cucumber and 1 chopped tomato. In a small bowl, mix together 2 tablespoons lemon juice, 1 crushed garlic clove and 2 tablespoons extra virgin olive oil; add to the salad with the burghul. Season with sea salt and freshly ground black pepper and toss to combine. Slice 1 Turkish bread loaf into 4 equal portions, then slice each horizontally through the centre. Toast each piece of bread, then spread one half generously with baba ghanoush. Add the rissole to the other bread halves. Top with the tabouleh and the other bread half and serve.

2 tablespoons olive oil, plus extra, for drizzling
1 onion, finely diced
3 garlic cloves, crushed
2 teaspoons ground coriander
1 teaspoon ground allspice
1 teaspoon sweet paprika
1 teaspoon ground turmeric
1 kg (2 lb 4 oz) minced (ground) lamb
1 egg, lightly beaten
80 g (2¾ oz/½ cup) pine nuts, toasted
1 small handful mint leaves, chopped
2 tablespoons tomato paste (concentrated purée)
150 g (5½ oz) mixed salad leaves
¼ red onion, thinly sliced
250 g (9 oz/1 cup) baba ghanoush

Preheat the oven to 180°C (350°F/Gas 4).

Heat half the olive oil in a large frying pan over low heat. Add the onion and garlic and sauté for 5 minutes, or until softened. Add the ground spices and cook, stirring, for 2 minutes, or until fragrant. Set aside to cool.

Place the lamb in a bowl with the egg, pine nuts, mint and tomato paste. Season with sea salt and freshly ground black pepper and mix until well combined. Add the cooked onion mixture. Mix well, then shape into 16 rissoles.

Heat the remaining oil in a large frying pan over medium heat. Add the rissoles, in batches if necessary, and cook for 4 minutes on each side, or until browned.

Transfer the rissoles to a large baking dish and bake for 8–10 minutes, or until cooked through.

For the next day, reserve half the rissoles for the Turkish bread sandwiches. (The rissoles can be refrigerated in an airtight container for up to 4 days, or frozen for up to 3 weeks.)

Place the salad leaves in a bowl with the red onion. Drizzle with extra olive oil and toss well to combine.

Serve the remaining rissoles with the salad and baba ghanoush.

Preparation time: 20 minutes   **Cooking time:** 35 minutes   **Serves:** 4

Preparation time: 20 minutes
plus 20 minutes soaking

Cooking time: 10 minutes

Serves: 4

Chinese-style turkey stir-fry

25 g (1 oz/1 cup) dried sliced shiitake
  mushrooms
100 g (3½ oz) dried bean thread noodles
1 teaspoon cornflour (cornstarch)
2 tablespoons oyster sauce
1 tablespoon Chinese chilli garlic sauce
1 tablespoon Chinese rice wine
2 teaspoons tomato sauce (ketchup)
1½ tablespoons peanut oil
1 carrot, cut into fine matchsticks
200 g (7 oz) green beans, trimmed and
  thinly sliced on the diagonal
4 spring onions (scallions), thinly sliced
  on the diagonal
1 tablespoon finely grated fresh ginger
300 g (10½ oz) minced (ground) turkey
300 g (10½ oz) Chinese cabbage,
  shredded
1 tablespoon soy sauce
150 g (5½ oz/1⅔ cups) bean sprouts,
  trimmed
1 large handful coriander (cilantro) leaves

Soak the shiitake mushrooms in a bowl of warm water for 20 minutes, or until softened. Drain well. Remove and discard the mushroom stalks, then thinly slice the caps.

Meanwhile, soak the noodles in cold water for 15 minutes, then drain well.

In a small bowl, mix the cornflour with 1 tablespoon cold water until smooth. Add the oyster sauce, chilli garlic sauce, rice wine and tomato sauce and set aside.

Heat half the peanut oil in a wok over high heat. Add the carrot, beans, spring onion and mushrooms and stir fry for 2–3 minutes, or until softened. Remove from the wok and set aside.

Add the remaining oil to the wok. Add the ginger and turkey and stir-fry for 3 minutes, breaking up any lumps with a fork.

Return the vegetables to the wok and add the cabbage and noodles. Stir-fry for 1–2 minutes, or until the cabbage has wilted.

For the next day, reserve about 2 cups of the stir-fry mixture for the turkey spring rolls. (The mixture can be refrigerated in an airtight container for up to 2 days, but is not suitable for freezing.)

Add the oyster sauce mixture to the remaining stir-fry and cook until heated through. Remove from the heat, add the soy sauce, bean sprouts and coriander and toss to combine. Serve immediately.

Turkey spring rolls
Serves 4 (makes 12)

Put the reserved turkey stir-fry mixture in a bowl with 2 teaspoons light soy sauce, 1 teaspoon kecap manis and a few drops of sesame oil and mix well. Lay 1 spring roll wrapper on a work surface and brush the edges with water. Place 1 heaped tablespoon of the mixture along the bottom half of the wrapper. Take the bottom edge and enclose the filling, tuck in the two side edges, then roll up firmly. Seal the edges. Repeat to make 12 spring rolls. Pour enough oil into a wok to deep-fry the spring rolls and heat to 180°C (350°F), or until a cube of bread dropped into the oil browns in 15 seconds. Deep-fry the spring rolls in batches until golden and crisp. Serve hot, with a small bowl of hoisin sauce thinned with a little hot water.

Carrot and feta omelette
Serves 4

Preheat the oven to 180°C (350°F/Gas 4). Grate 400 g (14 oz) sebago potatoes and squeeze out any excess liquid. Heat 30 g (1 oz) butter in a 22 cm (8½ inch) ovenproof frying pan over medium heat. Press the grated potato over the base of the pan and cook without stirring for 5 minutes, or until light golden underneath. Scatter the reserved braised carrots and 75 g (2½ oz/ ½ cup) crumbled feta cheese over the potato, then pour in 6 lightly beaten eggs. Transfer the pan to the oven and bake for 15–20 minutes, or until the egg has set. Turn the omelette out onto a plate and serve with a salad.

Steak with spiced braised carrots

2 tablespoons olive oil

2 red onions, cut into wedges

2 teaspoons ground cumin

2 teaspoons fennel seeds

1 teaspoon ground turmeric

a large pinch of saffron threads

2 tablespoons honey

3 wide orange zest strips

1.5 kg (3 lb 5 oz) carrots, quartered lengthways

250 ml (9 fl oz/1 cup) chicken stock

60 ml (2 fl oz/¼ cup) orange juice

155 g (5½ oz/1 cup) pitted green olives

4 x 150 g (5½ oz) skirt or minute steaks

100 g (3½ oz) baby green beans, trimmed

1 small handful coriander (cilantro) leaves, chopped

45 g (1½ oz/½ cup) toasted flaked almonds

Preheat the oven to 180°C (350°F/Gas 4).

Heat half the olive oil in a large flameproof baking dish over medium–high heat. Add the onion and sauté for 5 minutes, or until browned lightly. Add the spices and cook, stirring, for 1 minute, or until fragrant.

Add the honey, orange zest strips and carrots and stir to coat the carrots in the spices. Pour in the stock, orange juice and 125 ml (4 fl oz/½ cup) water and bring to the boil.

Cover the dish tightly with foil and bake for 40 minutes. Remove the foil and bake for another 30 minutes, or until the carrots are tender. Stir in the olives.

Just before serving, heat the remaining oil in a large frying pan over medium–high heat. Add the steaks and cook for 1–2 minutes on each side, or until done to your liking. Transfer to a plate and cover with foil to keep warm.

Meanwhile, cook the beans in a small saucepan of boiling salted water for 3 minutes, or until tender. Drain well.

For the next day, reserve 400 g (14 oz/2 cups) of the braised carrots for the carrot and feta omelette. (The carrots can be refrigerated in an airtight container for up to 2 days, but are not suitable for freezing.)

Divide the steaks, braised carrots and beans among serving plates. Serve sprinkled with the coriander and flaked almonds.

Preparation time: 15 minutes ✻ **Cooking time:** 1 hour 20 minutes ✻ **Serves:** 4

Preparation time: 20 minutes
plus 2 hours marinating

Cooking time: 20 minutes

Serves: 6

Teriyaki chicken with rice and vegetables

1.25 kg (2 lb 12 oz) chicken thigh
    fillets, trimmed and cut into strips
    2 cm (¾ inch) thick
200 ml (7 fl oz) teriyaki marinade
400 g (14 oz/2 cups) jasmine rice
60 ml (2 fl oz/¼ cup) vegetable oil
2 teaspoons sesame oil
1 garlic clove, crushed
1 tablespoon finely grated fresh ginger
4 spring onions (scallions), cut into
    long thin strips
1 carrot, cut into thin matchsticks
150 g (5½ oz/1 punnet) oyster
    mushrooms
8 baby corn, about 100 g (3½ oz)
12 snow peas (mangetout), trimmed
1 tablespoon sesame seeds

Place the chicken in a bowl. Add the teriyaki marinade and toss to coat. Cover and refrigerate for at least 2 hours. Drain well, reserving the marinade.

Preheat the oven to 150°C (300°F/Gas 2).

Rinse the rice until the water runs clear. Place in a saucepan with 450 ml (15½ fl oz) water. Bring to the boil and boil for 1 minute. Cover tightly, reduce the heat to as low as possible and cook for 10 minutes. Remove from the heat and leave to stand, covered, for 10 minutes.

Meanwhile, heat a wok over high heat. Add 1 tablespoon of the vegetable oil and swirl to coat the side. Add the chicken in batches and cook for 4–5 minutes, or until light golden and just cooked through, turning often.

For the next day, reserve one-third of the teriyaki chicken and 185 g (6½ oz/1 cup) of the steamed rice for the inari pockets. (The ingredients can be refrigerated in airtight containers for up to 2 days, but are not suitable for freezing.)

Transfer the remaining chicken to a baking dish. Cover with foil and keep warm in the oven.

Heat the sesame oil and remaining vegetable oil in the wok. Add the garlic, ginger, spring onion, carrot, mushrooms, baby corn and snow peas and stir-fry for 2–3 minutes, or until the vegetables are starting to soften.

Add the remaining chicken and all the reserved marinade. Cook, tossing, for 1–2 minutes, or until the liquid boils.

Serve the teriyaki chicken with the rice, sprinkled with the sesame seeds.

Inari pockets with teriyaki chicken
Serves 4 (makes 12)

Finely slice the reserved teriyaki chicken and add to a bowl with 2 tablespoons teriyaki marinade and the reserved rice. Add 90 g (3¼ oz/1 cup) blanched, cooled bean sprouts and 2 tablespoons chopped coriander (cilantro) and toss. In another bowl combine 2 teaspoons sesame oil, 1 tablespoon caster (superfine) sugar, 2 teaspoons soy sauce, 4 thinly sliced spring onions (scallions), 2 teaspoons mirin, 1 teaspoon crushed ginger and 2 teaspoons vegetable oil. Stir until the sugar has dissolved, then add to the chicken mixture and toss until well combined. Carefully spoon the mixture into 12 inari (Japanese tofu pockets). Serve immediately.

Sausage rolls
Serves 4 (makes 8)

Preheat the oven to 220°C (425°F/ Gas 7). Thaw 1 frozen puff pastry sheet and cut it in half lengthways. Place half the reserved lamb mixture down the centre of each sheet in a neat, long sausage shape. Roll the pastry up around the filling, brushing the edges lightly with beaten egg yolk to seal. Cut each roll into 4 even lengths. Place on a baking tray, seam side down, and bake for 20 minutes, or until the pastry is golden and crisp. Serve hot, with mango chutney.

Curried lamb skewers with rocket, tomato and coriander salad

1 kg (2 lb 4 oz) minced (ground) lamb
1 onion, finely chopped
2 long green chillies, finely chopped
3 garlic cloves, crushed
90 g (3¼ oz/⅓ cup) korma curry paste
65 g (2¼ oz/½ cup) pistachio nuts, finely chopped
2 tablespoons chopped flat-leaf (Italian) parsley, plus extra, to garnish
lemon wedges, to serve
olive oil, for brushing

Cumin-spiced onion
3 teaspoons cumin seeds
30 g (1 oz) butter
3 onions, thinly sliced

Rocket, tomato and coriander salad
100 g (3½ oz) rocket (arugula)
250 g (9 oz) cherry tomatoes, halved
1 Lebanese (short) cucumber, thinly sliced
1 small handful coriander (cilantro) leaves
2 tablespoons lemon juice
80 ml (2½ fl oz/⅓ cup) olive oil

Place the lamb in a large bowl with the onion, chilli, garlic, curry paste, pistachios and parsley. Season with sea salt and freshly ground black pepper and mix well.

For the next day, reserve about 2 cups of the lamb mixture for the sausage rolls. (The mixture can be refrigerated in an airtight container for up to 2 days, but is not suitable for freezing.)

Shape the remaining lamb mixture into 8 patties. Mould each portion around a metal skewer to make a 7.5 cm (3 inch) sausage shape. Refrigerate for 30 minutes to firm slightly.

To make the cumin-spiced onion, heat a non-stick frying pan over medium–low heat, add the cumin seeds and dry-fry for 2 minutes, or until fragrant, shaking the pan often. Tip the cumin seeds onto a plate.

Melt the butter in the pan over medium heat, then add the onion and sauté for 10 minutes, or until light golden. Add the cumin seeds, stir well to combine, then cook for another 2 minutes, or until fragrant.

Meanwhile, heat a chargrill pan or large frying pan until hot. Brush the lamb skewers with olive oil, add to the pan and fry in batches for 8 minutes, or until deep golden and cooked through, turning often.

In a bowl, toss together the rocket, tomato and coriander salad ingredients. Sprinkle the lamb skewers with extra parsley and serve with the cumin-spiced onion and salad.

✳ **Preparation time:** 20 minutes
plus 30 minutes chilling
✳ **Cooking time:** 25 minutes
✳ **Serves:** 4

Preparation time: 15 minutes   **Cooking time:** 1 hour 10 minutes   **Serves:** 6

Chicken with tomato, fennel and lemon

80 ml (2½ fl oz/⅓ cup) olive oil
6 chicken leg quarters (or 6 drumsticks
    and 6 thigh cutlets), trimmed of
    excess fat
2 onions, thinly sliced
3 garlic cloves, crushed
1 fennel bulb, thinly sliced
1.3 kg (3 lb) roma (plum) tomatoes,
    roughly chopped
1 teaspoon ground fennel seeds
2 teaspoons finely grated lemon rind
100 ml (3½ fl oz) lemon juice
250 ml (9 fl oz/1 cup) chicken stock
1 kg (2 lb 4 oz) new potatoes, scrubbed
    and halved
steamed spinach, to serve

Preheat the oven to 180°C (350°F/Gas 4).

Heat 1½ tablespoons of the olive oil in
a large heavy-based frying pan over medium
heat. Add the chicken in batches and cook for
3 minutes on each side, or until golden. Remove
to a plate.

Heat another 1½ tablespoons of oil in the
pan. Add the onion, garlic and fennel and sauté
for 6–8 minutes, or until the onion is very soft.
Add the tomatoes, fennel seeds and lemon rind,
then stir in the lemon juice and stock.

Return the chicken to the pan and bring to
the boil. Reduce the heat to low and simmer for
6 minutes, or until the tomatoes start to collapse.

Transfer the chicken to a large baking dish,
pour the tomato mixture over, then cover with
foil. Place the potatoes in a roasting tin with the
remaining oil, tossing to coat. Season with sea
salt and freshly ground black pepper.

Transfer the chicken and potatoes to the
oven. Bake for 15 minutes, then remove the foil
from the chicken. Bake for another 20 minutes,
or until the chicken is cooked through and the
potatoes are tender.

For the next day, reserve 810 ml (28 fl oz/
3¼ cups) of the tomato sauce for the fusilli. (The
sauce can be refrigerated in an airtight container
for up to 2 days, but is not suitable for freezing.)

Place the chicken on serving plates and spoon
the remaining tomato sauce over. Serve with the
roasted potatoes and steamed spinach.

Fusilli with spiced tomato sauce and omelette
Serves 4

Whisk 8 eggs in a bowl and season
with sea salt and ground white
pepper. Heat 1 teaspoon olive oil
in a large non-stick frying pan
over medium heat. Add one-third
of the egg mixture and cook for
5 minutes, or until firm and light
golden; remove to a chopping
board. Cook the remaining
egg in the same way to make
3 omelettes. Cut the omelettes
into 1 cm (½ inch) strips and set
aside. Heat 1 tablespoon olive oil
in the pan. Add 100 g (3½ oz)
thinly sliced prosciutto and fry
for 5 minutes, or until crisp. Add
the reserved tomato sauce and
simmer for 3 minutes, or until
heated through. Meanwhile, add
400 g (14 oz) fusilli to a large
pot of rapidly boiling salted water
and cook according to the packet
instructions until al dente. Drain
well, then add to the tomato sauce
with 80 g (2¾ oz/½ cup) thawed
frozen peas, 1 small handful
shredded basil and 1 small handful
flat-leaf (Italian) parsley. Divide
among bowls, top with the omelette
strips and serve.

Warm sausage and vegetable salad

Serves 4–6

Preheat the oven to 180°C (350°F/Gas 4). Wrap 500 g (1 lb 2 oz) trimmed, scrubbed baby beetroot (beets) in foil and place on a baking tray. Roast for 30 minutes, or until softened. (You can also use larger beetroot; they will take up to 1 hour 20 minutes to cook.) When cool enough to handle, peel the beetroot and cut in half (or cut larger ones into wedges). Thickly slice the reserved sausages and toss in a large bowl with the reserved roasted vegetables, 2 handfuls baby English spinach leaves and 2 segmented oranges. Arrange the salad and beetroot on serving plates. Mix the reserved currant anchovy relish with 2 tablespoons olive oil and 1 tablespoon red wine vinegar and drizzle over each salad. Top each with 1 teaspoon crème fraiche or sour cream and serve.

Italian pork sausages with currant anchovy relish and roast vegetables

2 eggplants (aubergine), about 800 g (1 lb 12 oz) in total, trimmed and cut widthways into 2 cm (¾ inch) slices
6 zucchini (courgettes), cut lengthways into slices 1 cm (½ inch) thick
olive oil, for brushing
16 thin Italian pork sausages, about 1.25 kg (2 lb 12 oz) in total
150 g (5½ oz) mixed salad leaves

Currant anchovy relish
1 tablespoon olive oil
1 onion, finely chopped
1 garlic clove, crushed
4 anchovy fillets, finely chopped
1 teaspoon finely grated orange rind
75 g (2½ oz/½ cup) currants
1 tablespoon red wine vinegar
400 g (14 oz) tin chopped tomatoes
2 tablespoons orange juice
150 g (5 oz) cherry tomatoes

Dressing
80 ml (2½ oz/⅓ cup) extra virgin olive oil
2 tablespoons red wine vinegar
1 small garlic clove, crushed
1 teaspoon dijon mustard

Preheat the oven to 200°C (400°F/Gas 6).

Grease 2 large baking trays and line with baking paper. Brush the eggplant and zucchini on both sides with olive oil, then arrange on the baking trays in a single layer. Season with sea salt and freshly ground black pepper and roast for 20 minutes. Remove the zucchini from the oven and roast the eggplant for another 10 minutes, or until tender.

Meanwhile, make the currant anchovy relish. Heat the olive oil in a small saucepan over medium heat. Add the onion and sauté for 6–7 minutes, or until softened. Add the garlic, anchovy and orange rind and cook, stirring, for 1 minute. Add the currants and vinegar. Stir for another minute, then add the tomatoes, orange juice and 125 ml (4 fl oz/½ cup) water. Bring to a simmer, then reduce the heat to low and cook for 15 minutes, or until reduced and slightly thickened. Add the cherry tomatoes and cook for 5 minutes, or until very slightly softened. Remove the relish from the heat and allow to cool slightly.

Heat a large lightly oiled frying pan over medium–high heat. Add the sausages, in batches if necessary, and cook for 10 minutes, or until well browned and cooked through, turning often.

Meanwhile, combine all the dressing ingredients in a bowl and whisk well. Season to taste and set aside.

For the next day, reserve 400 g (14 oz) of the roasted vegetables, 8 cooked sausages and 2 tablespoons of the currant anchovy relish for the warm sausage and vegetable salad. (The ingredients can be refrigerated in airtight containers for up to 2 days, but are not suitable for freezing.)

Toss the remaining roasted eggplant and zucchini with the mixed salad leaves, drizzle the dressing over and toss to combine. Serve with the sausages and currant anchovy relish.

Preparation time: 15 minutes
plus 2 hours marinating

Cooking time: 10 minutes

Serves: 4

Tofu skewers with peanut sauce

2 tablespoons kecap manis
2 tablespoons soy sauce
4 garlic cloves, crushed
1 teaspoon grated fresh ginger
1 tablespoon peanut oil
2 teaspoons ground cumin
2 teaspoons ground coriander
2 teaspoons sweet chilli sauce
700 g (1 lb 9 oz) firm tofu, drained
  and cut into 2 cm (¾ inch) chunks
250 g (9 oz) cherry tomatoes, halved
steamed brown rice, to serve

Peanut sauce

1 teaspoon peanut oil
2 garlic cloves, crushed
250 g (9 oz/1 cup) crunchy peanut butter
2 tablespoons fish sauce
125 ml (4 fl oz/½ cup) coconut milk

Combine the kecap manis, soy sauce, garlic, ginger, peanut oil, cumin, coriander and sweet chilli sauce in a bowl and stir to combine. Reserve 2 tablespoons of the marinade for the peanut sauce.

Add the tofu to the bowl and gently toss to coat. Cover and marinate in the refrigerator for 2 hours. Meanwhile, soak 12 wooden skewers in cold water for 30 minutes to prevent scorching.

To make the peanut sauce, heat the peanut oil in a small saucepan over low heat. Add the garlic and sauté for 2 minutes, then add the peanut butter, fish sauce, coconut milk, reserved marinade and 125 ml (4 fl oz/½ cup) water. Stir well, then heat slowly until hot.

For the next day, remove half the tofu from the marinade and reserve for the gado gado with half the peanut sauce. (The tofu should only be refrigerated for up to 24 hours; the peanut sauce can be refrigerated in an airtight container for up to 4 days, but is not suitable for freezing.)

Preheat the grill (broiler) to medium. Remove the remaining tofu from the marinade and drain well, reserving the marinade for basting. Thread the tofu chunks and cherry tomato halves onto each skewer.

Grill (broil) the skewers for 4 minutes on each side, or until browned, basting with the reserved marinade and turning during cooking. Serve with the remaining peanut sauce and steamed brown rice.

Gado gado
Serves 4

Heat 1 tablespoon peanut oil in a small frying pan over medium heat. Add the reserved tofu and cook until golden brown, turning often; set aside to cool. Place 6 small new potatoes in a saucepan, cover with cold water and boil for 12 minutes, or until tender; drain, cool and cut in half. Place 2 eggs in a small saucepan of cold water, bring to the boil and cook for 6 minutes, then place in a bowl of cold water to cool. Peel the eggs and cut into quarters lengthways. Bring another large saucepan of water to the boil. Add 1 thinly sliced carrot and 200 g (7 oz) trimmed green beans and cook for 4 minutes, then remove with a slotted spoon and plunge into a bowl of iced water. Add 200 g (7 oz/1⅔ cups) sliced Chinese cabbage to the saucepan, cook for 2 minutes, then plunge into the iced water. Drain well. Arrange the vegetables and eggs on a platter, top with the tofu, drizzle with the reheated reserved peanut sauce and serve.

Winter

Roast lamb with broad bean, mint and pea purée • Soy-braised chicken with Chinese mushrooms • Roast beef with harissa chickpea braise • Pork chops with creamed corn and asparagus • Persian beef with lentils and spinach • Pumpkin, bacon and parmesan risotto • Roast pork with apples and rosemary jus • Lamb stifado • Italian sweet and sour braised veal • Pork cutlets with fennel pancetta stuffing • Bolognese ragù • Beef and beer stew with carrot caraway mash • Greek bean stew with fried haloumi • Mushroom, red wine and barley risotto • Hearty pea and ham soup • Chicken, leek and bacon casserole • Lamb shanks with chorizo, mushrooms and buttered rice • Corned beef with braised cabbage • Lamb chops with crushed potatoes, capers and feta • Sausages with polenta and broccoli • Fish with olive oil mash and crisp pancetta • Saffron chicken with green olives and sweet potato • Tex-Mex bollito misto • Roast chicken tenderloins in pancetta with cauliflower purée • Pork and prune meatloaf with balsamic onion sauce • Chinese pork noodles • Tandoori roast chicken • Silverbeet, chickpea and almond tagine • Steamed snapper with burghul pilaff and pine nut sauce • Slow-roasted lamb with honey pomegranate onion jam • Chicken and leek pie • Smoked fish with horseradish cream sauce • Pot roast Indian lamb • Risoni, beef and walnut pilaff • Lamb cutlets with spicy red lentils • Beef in red wine with prunes and dark chocolate • Ginger and star anise braised pork • Roast chicken with lemon, honey, rosemary and zucchini • Warm vegetable and lentil salad • Roasted ham with sweet potato and mustard fruits • Lamb steaks with white bean and potato ragoût • Classic meatballs • Indian curried lamb • Chorizo and capsicum paella • Stuffed chicken thighs with pancetta • Veal and vegetable stew with buttered noodles • Rustic fish stew • Lamb, raisin and orange pilaff

Lamb, pumpkin and capsicum salad with sweet balsamic dressing
Serves 4

Bring the reserved lamb, pumpkin and onions to room temperature. Meanwhile, cut a large red capsicum (pepper) into strips 2 cm (¾ inch) wide. Brush the capsicum with olive oil and chargrill or barbecue for 6–7 minutes, or until tender and charred all over, turning occasionally. Cool slightly and place in a large bowl. Carve the lamb into thin slices and add to the bowl with the pumpkin, onion, 1 handful rocket (arugula) and 1 handful mint. Add a few kalamata olives if you like. Drizzle with extra virgin olive oil and balsamic vinegar and toss gently to combine. Divide among bowls and serve.

Roast lamb with broad bean, mint and pea purée

2.7 kg (6 lb) leg of lamb, trimmed
   of excess fat
6 onions, peeled leaving the root end
   intact, then quartered lengthways
60 ml (2 fl oz/¼ cup) olive oil
1.4 kg (3 lb 2 oz) butternut pumpkin
   (squash), cut into 4 cm (1½ inch)
   chunks
1 tablespoon balsamic vinegar or
   balsamic vinegar glaze

Broad bean, mint and pea purée
1 teaspoon sea salt
300 g (10½ oz/2 cups) frozen broad
   (fava) beans, thawed and peeled
300 g (10½ oz/2 cups) frozen peas
40 g (1½ oz) unsalted butter
1½ tablespoons chopped mint

Preheat the oven to 180°C (350°F/Gas 4).

Season the lamb all over with sea salt and freshly ground black pepper. Place on a roasting rack in a large flameproof roasting tin and roast for 40 minutes.

Spread the onions in another large roasting tin and drizzle with the olive oil. Transfer to the oven and roast with the lamb for another 40 minutes.

Turn the onions over, add the pumpkin to the same roasting tin, then roast for a final 30 minutes, or until the lamb is just cooked through and the vegetables are very tender.

Remove the lamb from the oven, cover with foil and rest in a warm place for 10 minutes. Keep the vegetables warm in the oven.

Put the roasting tin with the pan juices on the stovetop over medium heat. Stir in the vinegar and simmer for 5 minutes, or until reduced.

Meanwhile, make the broad bean, mint and pea purée. Bring 625 ml (21½ fl oz/2½ cups) water to the boil in a small saucepan with the sea salt. Add the broad beans and peas, then cover and simmer over medium heat for 5 minutes, or until tender. Using a slotted spoon, transfer the beans and peas to a food processor, with 80 ml (2½ fl oz/⅓ cup) of the cooking liquid. Process until a smooth purée forms, then return to the saucepan. Stir in the butter and season to taste. Keep warm until ready to serve. Just before serving, stir in the mint.

For the next day, reserve half the lamb, half the pumpkin and half the onions for the lamb, pumpkin and capsicum salad. (The ingredients can be refrigerated in airtight containers for up to 3 days, but are not suitable for freezing.)

Carve the remaining lamb and divide among serving plates with the remaining pumpkin and onions. Drizzle with the balsamic gravy and serve with the broad bean, mint and pea purée.

Preparation time: 40 minutes   **Cooking time:** 2 hours   **Serves:** 4

Preparation time: 20 minutes   **Cooking time:** 1 hour   **Serves:** 4

Soy-braised chicken with Chinese mushrooms

500 ml (17 fl oz/2 cups) Chinese rice
wine or dry sherry
1 litre (35 fl oz/4 cups) chicken stock
250 ml (9 fl oz/1 cup) light soy sauce
175 g (6 oz/½ cup) honey
55 g (2 oz/¼ cup) sliced fresh ginger
4 garlic cloves, quartered
2 star anise
2.5 kg (5 lb 8 oz) chicken leg quarters,
trimmed of excess fat, backbones
removed
2 tablespoons peanut oil
200 g (7 oz) oyster mushrooms
200 g (7 oz) shiitake mushrooms
2 teaspoons sesame oil
2 spring onions (scallions), cut into
thin strips
steamed rice, to serve

Combine the wine, stock, soy sauce, honey, ginger, garlic and star anise in a large heavy-based saucepan. Bring the mixture to the boil, then reduce the heat to low. Simmer, uncovered, for 10 minutes.

Add the chicken to the liquid, then cover and simmer over very low heat for 40 minutes. Do not allow bubbles to break the surface — the chicken will be tough if the mixture simmers too hard.

Remove the chicken from the cooking liquid, reserving 500 ml (17 fl oz/2 cups) of the broth. Discard the remaining liquid, or cool and freeze for use as a stock. Keep warm.

For the next day, reserve 2 chicken portions and 250 ml (9 fl oz/1 cup) of the reserved cooking broth for the chicken and snow pea won tons. (The ingredients can be refrigerated in airtight containers for up to 3 days, but are not suitable for freezing.)

Heat the peanut oil in a large frying pan over high heat. Add the mushrooms and sauté for 3 minutes, or until lightly browned. Add the sesame oil, season to taste with sea salt and freshly ground black pepper and toss to combine.

Cut the remaining chicken portions into two pieces each. Serve on a bed of steamed rice, with the mushrooms, spring onion and the remaining reserved cooking broth spooned over the top.

Chicken and snow pea won tons with salad
Serves 4

Remove the meat from the reserved chicken pieces, discarding the skin and bones. Place the chicken meat in a food processor with 3 teaspoons finely chopped fresh ginger, 1 chopped spring onion (scallion) and 1 egg and blend to a coarse paste. Stir in 70 g (2½ oz/¾ cup) finely chopped snow peas (mangetout). Place a won ton wrapper on a work surface and top with 2 teaspoons of the chicken mixture. Brush two edges with water, then fold over to enclose the filling. Repeat with more won ton wrappers and the remaining chicken mixture to make 20 won tons. Cook the won tons, in batches, in a saucepan of salted boiling water. Meanwhile, heat the reserved chicken cooking broth. In a bowl, quickly toss together 1 small handful picked watercress, 1 handful coriander (cilantro) leaves, 1 small handful trimmed snow pea (mangetout) sprouts and 75 g (2½ oz/1 cup) shredded Chinese cabbage. Place 5 won tons in each serving bowl, ladle the broth over, scatter with the salad and serve.

Roast beef with harissa chickpea braise

Beef, tomato and chickpea soup
Serves 4

Chop 1 eggplant (aubergine) and 1 onion into 2 cm (¾ inch) cubes. Heat 2 tablespoons vegetable oil in a large saucepan over medium heat. Add the eggplant and onion and sauté for 5–7 minutes, or until the eggplant has softened slightly. Chop the reserved roast beef into small pieces and add to the pan with 1 tablespoon of the reserved harissa. Fry for 1 minute, then add the reserved chickpea braise, 500 ml (17 fl oz/2 cups) water and 500 ml (17 fl oz/2 cups) beef stock. Bring to the boil, then reduce the heat to low, cover and simmer for 1–1½ hours, or until the beef is very tender. Add 2 tablespoons chopped coriander (cilantro), season to taste with sea salt and freshly ground black pepper and serve.

2 tablespoons vegetable oil
1.5 kg (3 lb 5 oz) beef sirloin roast
1 onion, finely diced
1 leek, white part only, rinsed well and finely diced
1 red capsicum (pepper), cut into 2 cm (¾ inch) pieces
400 g (14 oz) tin chickpeas, rinsed and drained
600 ml (21 fl oz) jar tomato passata (puréed tomatoes)
300 g (10½ oz) green beans, trimmed

Harissa
200 g (7 oz) jar roasted capsicums (peppers), drained
3 garlic cloves, roughly chopped
3 coriander (cilantro) roots, washed well and chopped
1 tablespoon caraway seeds
2 tablespoons mint, chopped
1 small red chilli, chopped
60 ml (2 fl oz/¼ cup) extra virgin olive oil

Preheat the oven to 170°C (325°F/Gas 3).

Heat 1 tablespoon of the oil in a flameproof roasting tin over medium heat. Add the beef and cook for 5–6 minutes, or until browned all over, turning often. Season well with sea salt and freshly ground black pepper, then transfer to the oven and roast for 1¼ hours.

Meanwhile, make the harissa. Combine the capsicum, garlic, coriander root, caraway seeds, mint, chilli and some sea salt in a food processor and blend to a rough paste. With the motor running, add the olive oil and blend to a purée. Season to taste and set aside.

While the beef is roasting, heat the remaining oil in a saucepan over medium heat. Add the onion and leek and sauté for 4–5 minutes, or until softened but not coloured. Add the capsicum and cook for another 2 minutes. Add 2 tablespoons of the harissa, the chickpeas and the tomato passata. Bring to the boil, then reduce the heat and simmer for 10–15 minutes, or until thickened slightly.

Bring a saucepan of water to the boil over high heat. Quickly blanch the beans for 3 minutes, or until just tender. Drain.

For the next day, reserve about 300 g (10½ oz) of the beef, about 2 cups of the chickpea braise and some harissa for the beef, tomato and chickpea soup. (The ingredients can be refrigerated in airtight containers for up to 3 days, but are not suitable for freezing.)

Carve the remaining roast beef and serve with the beans and remaining chickpea braise, with some of the remaining harissa passed separately.

✳ **Preparation time:** 20 minutes   ✳ **Cooking time:** 1 hour 20 minutes   ✳ **Serves:** 4

Preparation time: 15 minutes   **Cooking time:** 35 minutes   **Serves:** 4

Pork chops with creamed corn and asparagus

30 g (1 oz) butter

1 large leek, white part only, rinsed well and thinly sliced

2 garlic cloves, crushed

1 tablespoon plain (all-purpose) flour

1 kg (2 lb 4 oz) frozen corn kernels, thawed

250 ml (9 fl oz/1 cup) chicken stock

250 ml (9 fl oz/1 cup) cream

60 ml (2 fl oz/¼ cup) olive oil

2 teaspoons finely grated lemon rind

3 tablespoons sweet paprika

2 teaspoons smoked paprika

6 x 200 g (7 oz) pork loin chops

350 g (12 oz/2 bunches) asparagus spears, trimmed

Melt the butter in a large heavy-based saucepan. Add the leek and garlic and sauté over medium heat for 5 minutes, or until softened.

Add the flour and cook, stirring, for 1–2 minutes. Add the corn, stock and cream and stir until well combined. Bring to a simmer over low heat, then cook for 20 minutes, stirring occasionally. Remove from the heat.

For the next day, reserve 250 g (9 oz/1 cup) of the creamed corn mixture for the corn and spring onion quiche. (The corn mixture can be refrigerated in an airtight container for up to 3 days, but is not suitable for freezing.)

Remove another 250 g (9 oz/1 cup) of the creamed corn and set aside. Using a food processor or blender, purée the remaining corn mixture until almost smooth, then return to the saucepan. Add the reserved 250 g (9 oz/1 cup) corn mixture and stir to combine and heat through. Keep warm.

Combine the olive oil, lemon rind and all the paprika in a bowl. Add the pork chops and toss to coat, then season with sea salt and freshly ground black pepper.

Place a large frying pan over medium–high heat. Cook the pork chops for 2–3 minutes on each side, or until cooked through. Transfer to a plate and cover with foil to keep warm.

Meanwhile, bring a saucepan of water to the boil over high heat. Add the asparagus and cook for 2 minutes, or until tender. Drain well.

Divide the pork chops among serving plates. Serve with the creamed corn and asparagus.

✳ Corn and spring onion quiche
Serves 6

Grease a 23 cm (9 inch) loose-based flan (tart) tin. Line the tin with 1½ sheets of thawed frozen shortcrust (pie) pastry, cutting and joining the pastry where necessary. Trim the edges, then chill the pastry for 30 minutes. Preheat the oven to 200°C (400°F/Gas 6). Place the flan tin on a baking tray. Line the pastry with baking paper, fill with dried beans, rice or baking beads and bake for 20 minutes. Remove the beans and baking paper and bake for another 5 minutes, then remove from the oven and cool slightly. Whisk 5 eggs and 125 ml (4 fl oz/½ cup) cream; season well with sea salt and freshly ground black pepper and set aside. Spread the reserved creamed corn over the pastry base, then sprinkle with 2 thinly sliced spring onions (scallions) and 60 g (2¼ oz/½ cup) grated cheddar cheese. Gently pour in the egg mixture and bake for 20 minutes, or until the quiche is lightly browned, cooked through and firm to the touch. Serve warm or cold, with a green salad.

Beef, pumpkin and pea pot pies
Serves 4 (makes 4)

Preheat the oven to 180ºC (350ºF/ Gas 4). Combine the reserved beef and pumpkin in a saucepan with 80 g (2¾ oz/½ cup) frozen peas. Bring to a gentle simmer over medium heat, then spoon into four 250 ml (9 fl oz/1 cup) ramekins. Take 4 filo pastry sheets and cut each into 8 even squares. Brush each generously with melted butter, then lightly crumple and arrange 8 squares over the top of each pie. Place on a baking tray and bake for 15–20 minutes, or until the pastry is golden. Serve immediately.

Persian beef with lentils and spinach

80 ml (2½ fl oz/⅓ cup) olive oil
1.75 kg (3 lb 14 oz) stewing steak, such as chuck, trimmed and cut into 4 cm (1½ inch) chunks
2 onions, thinly sliced
2 garlic cloves, thinly sliced
3 teaspoons ground turmeric
1½ tablespoons sweet paprika
60 ml (2 fl oz/¼ cup) tomato paste (concentrated purée)
1 tablespoon plain (all-purpose) flour
750 ml (26 fl oz/3 cups) beef stock
400 g (14 oz) tin chopped tomatoes
2 tablespoons honey
1.25 kg (2 lb 12 oz) pumpkin (winter squash), cut into 4 cm (1½ inch) chunks
400 g (14 oz) tin lentils, rinsed and drained
500 g (1 lb 2 oz/1 bunch) English spinach, trimmed and chopped
1½ tablespoons lime juice
steamed rice, to serve
coriander (cilantro) leaves, to garnish

Preheat the oven to 160ºC (315ºF/Gas 2–3).

Heat 2 tablespoons of the olive oil in a large flameproof casserole dish over high heat. Season the steak well with sea salt and freshly ground black pepper and sear in batches for 3–4 minutes, or until golden brown, turning often. Remove to a plate and set aside.

Reduce the heat to medium. Heat another 1 tablespoon olive oil in the dish. Add the onion and sauté for 5–6 minutes, or until softened.

Add the garlic, turmeric and paprika and cook, stirring, for 1 minute. Add the tomato paste and flour and cook for 30 seconds. Pour in 250 ml (9 fl oz/1 cup) of the stock and stir until thickened. Add the remaining stock, tomatoes, 1 tablespoon of the honey and all the beef and bring to a simmer. Cover, transfer to the oven and bake for 1 hour.

Place the pumpkin on a baking tray lined with baking paper. Drizzle with the remaining olive oil and honey and season well. Toss to coat, cover firmly with foil, then transfer to the oven with the beef and roast for 30 minutes.

Remove the foil from the pumpkin and bake for a further 30 minutes, or until the beef is very tender and the pumpkin is golden and tender.

For the next day, reserve about 3 cups of the beef casserole and one-quarter of the pumpkin for the pot pies. (The beef and pumpkin can be refrigerated in airtight containers for up to 3 days; the beef can also be frozen for up to 6 weeks.)

Stir the lentils, spinach and lime juice through the remaining beef casserole. Cover and bake for a further 5 minutes, or until the spinach has wilted. Season to taste.

Serve the beef and roasted pumpkin on a bed of steamed rice, scattered with coriander leaves.

Preparation time: 30 minutes **Cooking time:** 2 hours 30 minutes **Serves:** 4–6

Preparation time: 25 minutes   **Cooking time:** 35 minutes   **Serves:** 4

Pumpkin, bacon and parmesan risotto

4 rindless bacon slices, about 200 g
  (7 oz), cut into thin strips
400 g (14 oz) pumpkin (winter squash),
  cut into 1 cm (½ inch) pieces
1 thyme sprig
1.5 litres (52 fl oz/6 cups) chicken stock
2 tablespoons olive oil
1 large onion, finely chopped
2 garlic cloves, crushed
500 g (1 lb 2 oz/2¼ cups) arborio rice
250 ml (9 fl oz/1 cup) white wine
50 g (1¾ oz/½ cup) grated parmesan
1 handful flat-leaf (Italian) parsley,
  finely chopped

Preheat the oven to 180°C (350°F/Gas 4).

Line a baking tray with baking paper and add the bacon, pumpkin and thyme sprig. Season with sea salt and freshly ground black pepper and toss well. Bake for 30 minutes, or until the pumpkin is tender and the bacon is crisp. Pull the thyme leaves from the sprig and sprinkle over the pumpkin. Keep warm.

Meanwhile, heat the stock in a saucepan over medium heat. Keep at a low simmer.

In a separate heavy-based saucepan, heat the olive oil over medium heat. Add the onion and sauté for 10 minutes, or until translucent. Add the garlic and cook for a further 30 seconds, then add the rice and stir to coat. Pour in the wine, bring to a simmer, then cook for 3 minutes, or until the liquid has reduced by half.

Add 250 ml (9 fl oz/1 cup) of the simmering stock to the rice mixture, then cook, stirring, until the stock has been absorbed. Continue adding the stock, 250 ml (9 fl oz/1 cup) at a time, stirring until the stock has all been used and the rice is creamy and cooked, but still a little firm. (This should take about 20 minutes; do not overcook the rice as it will continue cooking upon standing.)

Remove the saucepan from the heat. Add the parmesan and stir to combine, then cover and leave to stand for 5 minutes.

For the next day, reserve 3 cups of the risotto for the blue cheese arancini. (The risotto can be refrigerated in an airtight container for up to 2 days, but is not suitable for freezing.)

Stir the pumpkin, bacon and parsley into the remaining risotto. Season to taste and serve.

Blue cheese arancini
Serves 4 (makes about 12)

Mix 1 egg into the chilled reserved risotto mixture until well combined. Place 100 g (3½ oz/1 cup) dry breadcrumbs on a large plate, and 75 g (2½ oz/½ cup) plain (all-purpose) flour in a bowl. In another bowl lightly whisk 2 eggs. Using wet hands, shape 2 tablespoons of the risotto into a ball. Press a 2 cm (¾ inch) piece of blue cheese into the centre of the ball and mould to enclose; you will need about 150 g (5½ oz) blue cheese altogether. Dip the ball into the flour, then the egg, then roll it in the breadcrumbs until well coated. Repeat with the remaining mixture and refrigerate until chilled. Heat about 5 cm (2 inches) of vegetable oil in a deep-fryer or large heavy-based saucepan to 180°C (350°F), or until a cube of bread dropped into the oil browns in 15 seconds. Cook the arancini in batches for 3–5 minutes, or until golden and heated through. Drain on kitchen paper and serve.

Latkes with goat's cheese and hazelnuts

Serves 4

Preheat the oven to 160°C (315°F/ Gas 2–3). Grate the reserved boiled potatoes and any leftover roast potatoes into a bowl. Add 1 egg, 1 small finely chopped onion, 2½ tablespoons fresh breadcrumbs, 1 teaspoon garlic salt and some ground white pepper. Mix well, then mould into tablespoon-sized patties. Heat 60 ml (2 fl oz/¼ cup) vegetable oil in a frying pan over medium heat. Fry the patties in batches for 5 minutes, or until golden; keep warm in the oven. Put some rocket (arugula) in a bowl, add 1 tablespoon balsamic vinegar and 2 tablespoons extra virgin olive oil, toss well and season to taste with sea salt and freshly ground black pepper. Serve the latkes with the salad, topped with the reserved apple sauce, some crumbled goat's cheese and 40 g (1½ oz/⅓ cup) chopped, roasted hazelnuts.

Roast pork with apples and rosemary jus

1.25 kg (2 lb 12 oz) rolled pork loin
2 tablespoons vegetable oil
2 teaspoons sea salt
1.25 kg (2 lb 12 oz) roasting potatoes, peeled and cut into 4 cm (1½ inch) chunks
4 granny smith apples, peeled, cored and cut into 8 wedges
2 tablespoons caster (superfine) sugar
1 tablespoon lemon juice
125 ml (4 fl oz/½ cup) red wine
1 rosemary sprig
1 tablespoon plain (all-purpose) flour
250 ml (9 fl oz/1 cup) beef stock

Preheat the oven to 200°C (400°F/Gas 6).

Place the pork in a roasting tin. Drizzle 1 tablespoon of the oil over the pork and rub in well. Sprinkle with half the sea salt, then place in the oven to roast for 1¼ hours.

Meanwhile, place the potatoes in a large saucepan and cover with cold water. Add the remaining sea salt and bring to the boil. Cook for 8 minutes, or until the potatoes are tender but still firm. Drain the potatoes well, reserving half for the latkes.

Place the remaining potatoes in the oven with the roasting pork. Baste the pork and potatoes with the pan juices and continue roasting.

Meanwhile, put the apples in a saucepan with the sugar, lemon juice and 125 ml (4 fl oz/½ cup) water. Bring to the boil, reduce to a simmer, then cook for 25 minutes, or until the apples have collapsed into a coarse purée (add more water if the apples become too dry).

For the next day, reserve half the apple sauce and half the boiled potatoes for the latkes. (The ingredients can be refrigerated in airtight containers for up to 3 days, but are not suitable for freezing.)

After the pork has roasted for 1¼ hours, remove it from the oven and test it with a skewer. The pork is ready when the juices run clear; if not, return it to the oven and roast a little longer.

When the pork is done, remove to a warm platter, cover with foil and rest in a warm place for 10 minutes. Place the potatoes in another large baking dish and keep warm in the oven.

Put the roasting tin with the pan juices on the stovetop over medium heat. Add the wine and rosemary sprig, bring to the boil and cook for 3–4 minutes, or until the liquid has reduced by half. Stir in the flour and add the stock. Simmer, stirring, until the jus is thickened and smooth.

Carve the pork and serve with the rosemary jus, roast potatoes and remaining apple sauce.

Preparation time: 30 minutes   **Cooking time:** 1 hour 25 minutes   **Serves:** 4

Lamb stifado

60 ml (2 fl oz/¼ cup) olive oil, plus
  extra for pan-frying, if necessary
600 g (1 lb 5 oz) pickling onions, peeled
1.8 kg (4 lb) boneless lamb shoulder
  or leg, trimmed and cut into 2 cm
  (¾ inch) chunks
4 garlic cloves, chopped
2 rosemary sprigs
1 tablespoon dried oregano
560 ml (19¼ fl oz/2¼ cups) red wine
375 ml (13 fl oz/1½ cups) chicken stock
2 cinnamon sticks
2 bay leaves
2 tablespoons red wine vinegar
2½ tablespoons tomato paste
  (concentrated purée)
2 x 400 g (14 oz) tins chopped tomatoes
35 g (1¼ oz/¼ cup) currants
crumbled feta, to serve
crusty bread, to serve

Heat the olive oil in a heavy-based saucepan over medium–low heat. Add the onions and sauté for 5–10 minutes, or until lightly browned. Remove to a plate using a slotted spoon and set aside.

Increase the heat to medium. Add the lamb to the pan and cook in batches for 3–5 minutes on each side, or until well browned, adding a little extra oil if necessary. Remove to a plate, reserving any pan juices.

Return all the meat, onions and any juices to the pan. Stir in the garlic, rosemary sprigs, oregano, wine, stock, cinnamon sticks, bay leaves, vinegar, tomato paste and tomatoes, then bring to a simmer. Season well with sea salt and freshly ground black pepper, then reduce the heat to low. Cover and cook for 1 hour, stirring occasionally.

Stir in the currants and cook for a further 15 minutes, then discard the cinnamon sticks.

For the next day, reserve one-quarter of the lamb and onions for the lamb pizzas. (The ingredients can be refrigerated in airtight containers for up to 3 days, but are not suitable for freezing.)

Serve the remaining stifado scattered with crumbled feta, with crusty bread.

Lamb pizzas with olives and garlic yoghurt sauce
Serves 4

Preheat the oven to 220°C (425°F/ Gas 7). Remove the lamb chunks from the reserved stifado, then simmer the sauce in a saucepan for 5 minutes, or until reduced and thickened. Place two 24 cm (9½ inch) pizza bases on baking trays and spread each with 1 tablespoon hummus. Arrange the reserved lamb and onions on each pizza, then drizzle with the reduced sauce. Scatter 155 g (5½ oz/1 cup) pitted kalamata olives and 200 g (7 oz/1⅓ cups) crumbled feta cheese over the pizzas, then some flat-leaf (Italian) parsley and oregano. Drizzle the pizzas with olive oil, then bake for 12–15 minutes, or until the bases are crisp and the tops are golden.

Veal pasta with eggplant and olives

Serves 4

Add 300 g (10½ oz) pappardelle to a large pot of rapidly boiling salted water and cook according to the packet instructions until al dente. Meanwhile, place the reserved veal in a large frying pan over medium heat. Add 200 g (7 oz) chopped marinated chargrilled eggplant (aubergine) and 60 g (2¼ oz/¼ cup) ligurian olives. Cook, stirring, for 5 minutes, or until heated through. Drain the pasta and add to the veal with some chopped flat-leaf (Italian) parsley. Gently toss together and serve with shaved parmesan if desired.

Italian sweet and sour braised veal

2.5 kg (5 lb 8 oz) veal osso buco
35 g (1¼ oz/¼ cup) plain (all-purpose) flour
60 ml (2 fl oz/¼ cup) olive oil
1 large onion, thinly sliced
1 large red capsicum (pepper), thinly sliced
2 garlic cloves, crushed
10 anchovies, chopped
2 tablespoons drained capers, chopped
40 g (1½ oz/⅓ cup) raisins, chopped
2 rosemary sprigs, plus extra, to garnish
60 ml (2 fl oz/¼ cup) red wine vinegar
2 tablespoons tomato paste (concentrated purée)
500 ml (17 fl oz/2 cups) beef stock
2 x 400 g (14 oz) tins chopped tomatoes
boiled potatoes, to serve
green beans, to serve
1 small handful flat-leaf (Italian) parsley

Dust the veal with the flour, shaking off any excess. Heat 2 tablespoons of the olive oil in a large flameproof casserole dish over medium heat. Add the veal in batches and cook for 5 minutes, or until browned all over, turning regularly. Remove to a plate.

Heat the remaining oil in the dish. Add the onion and capsicum and sauté over medium heat for 5 minutes, or until softened.

Add the garlic, anchovies, capers, raisins and rosemary sprigs. Cook, stirring, for 1 minute, then pour in the vinegar. Bring to the boil, reduce the heat to low and simmer for 3 minutes, or until the liquid has reduced by half.

Stir in the tomato paste, stock and tomatoes and bring to the boil. Reduce the heat to low, then return the veal to the pan. Cover and simmer for 1½ hours.

Remove the lid and simmer for another 1 hour, or until the veal is very tender. Using a slotted spoon, remove the veal to a warm platter, cover with foil and leave to rest in a warm place.

Return the cooking liquid to a simmer and cook for 20 minutes, or until reduced and thickened slightly. Discard the rosemary sprigs.

For the next day, reserve 600 g (1 lb 5 oz/ 3 cups) of the meat and sauce for the veal pasta. (The mixture can be refrigerated in an airtight container for up to 3 days, but is not suitable for freezing.)

Serve the veal with boiled potatoes and green beans, sprinkled with the parsley and extra rosemary sprigs.

Preparation time: 20 minutes   Cooking time: 3 hours 15 minutes   Serves: 4

Preparation time: 35 minutes   **Cooking time:** 55 minutes   **Serves:** 4

Pork cutlets with fennel pancetta stuffing

1.5 kg (3 lb 5 oz) floury potatoes,
  peeled and chopped
60 g (2¼ oz) butter
125 ml (4 fl oz/½ cup) milk, warmed
2 tablespoons olive oil
6 pancetta slices, about 80 g (2¾ oz)
  in total, finely chopped
1 small fennel bulb, about 200 g (7 oz),
  trimmed and very thinly sliced
1 teaspoon thyme
1 slice sourdough bread, torn into
  small pieces
375 ml (13 fl oz/1½ cups) beef stock
5 pork loin cutlets, about 225–250 g
  (8–9 oz) each
1 onion, thinly sliced
1 garlic clove, crushed
40 g (1½ oz/⅓ cup) raisins
60 ml (2 fl oz/¼ cup) white wine

Preheat the oven to 180°C (350°F/Gas 4).

Place the potatoes in a large saucepan and cover with cold water. Bring to the boil, then reduce the heat and simmer for 10–12 minutes, or until tender. Drain well, then return to the saucepan. Add two-thirds of the butter and all the warm milk and mash until smooth. Season to taste with sea salt and freshly ground black pepper. Cover and keep warm.

Meanwhile, heat half the olive oil in a small frying pan over medium heat. Add the pancetta, fennel and thyme and sauté for 6–8 minutes, or until the pancetta is golden and the fennel is tender. Remove from the heat. Add the bread pieces and just enough (1–2 tablespoons) of the stock to enable the mixture to hold together. Set aside to cool slightly.

Create a pocket in each pork cutlet by cutting into one side of each cutlet with a small sharp knife to make a cavity, taking care not to cut through the sides of the cutlets. Fill each pocket with the cooled pancetta mixture.

Heat a large heavy-based frying pan over high heat. Brush the cutlets with the remaining oil and season well. Cook in batches for 2–3 minutes on each side, then transfer to a baking tray and bake for 5–7 minutes, or until done to your liking. Remove from the oven, cover with foil and leave to rest in a warm place for 10 minutes.

For the next day, reserve 1 pork cutlet and 450 g (1 lb/2 cups) of the mashed potato for the pork and fennel hash. (The ingredients can be refrigerated in airtight containers for 1 day, but are not suitable for freezing.)

Return the frying pan to medium heat and add the remaining butter. Sauté the onion for 5 minutes, then add the garlic and cook for 1 minute. Add the raisins, pour in the wine and cook until reduced by half. Add the remaining stock and simmer gently for 5 minutes.

Serve the pork cutlets immediately, with the mashed potato and the raisin sauce.

Pork and fennel hash
Serves 4

Preheat the oven to 180°C (350°F/ Gas 4). Roughly chop the meat from the reserved pork cutlet and place in a bowl with the reserved mashed potato. Heat 10 g (¼ oz) butter and 1 teaspoon olive oil in an ovenproof frying pan over medium heat. Add 1 sliced onion and sauté for 7–10 minutes, or until golden and tender. Add 1 crushed garlic clove and cook for 1 minute, then add to the mashed potato along with 65 g (2½ oz/½ cup) grated gruyère cheese, 2 beaten eggs and 1 small handful chopped parsley. Season with sea salt and freshly ground black pepper and mix well. Heat another tablespoon of oil in the pan and press the mashed potato mixture over the base. Smooth the surface with a spatula. Transfer to the oven and bake for 15 minutes, or until the hash is golden and set. Cut into wedges and serve with a green salad.

Baked stuffed eggplants
Serves 4

Preheat the oven to 190°C (375°F/ Gas 5). Slice two 350 g (12 oz) eggplants (aubergine) in half lengthways. Drizzle generously with olive oil and season well with sea salt and freshly ground black pepper. Cover loosely with foil and bake for 45 minutes, or until tender when pierced with a knife. Meanwhile, melt 30 g (1 oz) butter in a small saucepan. Stir in 2½ tablespoons plain (all-purpose) flour and cook, stirring, for 1–2 minutes, or until smooth. Add 300 ml (10½ fl oz) milk, whisking constantly; bring to a simmer and continue whisking over low heat for 5 minutes, then season to taste. Remove the eggplant flesh from each eggplant half with a spoon, leaving a border of flesh 1 cm (½ inch) thick. Chop the flesh. Squeeze 1 tablespoon lemon juice over the eggplant shells and flesh. Stir the chopped eggplant flesh into the reserved ragù, then spoon the mixture back into the eggplant shells. Place them in a ceramic baking dish, spoon the white sauce over and sprinkle with grated cheddar cheese. Bake for 45 minutes, or until the eggplant is golden and tender.

Bolognese ragù

1½ tablespoons olive oil
1 large onion, finely chopped
1 celery stalk, finely chopped
1 carrot, finely chopped
6 anchovies, chopped
4 garlic cloves, crushed
2 thyme sprigs, plus extra, to garnish
1 kg (2 lb 4 oz) minced (ground) veal, not too lean
90 g (3¼ oz/1 cup) chopped Swiss brown mushrooms
100 g (3½ oz) tomato paste (concentrated purée)
200 ml (7 fl oz) white wine
2 x 400 g (14 oz) tins chopped tomatoes
2 bay leaves
1 small handful basil, torn
350 g (12 oz) spaghetti
50 g (1¾ oz/½ cup) shaved parmesan

Heat the olive oil in a large, heavy-based saucepan over medium heat. Reduce the heat to low, add the onion, celery and carrot and sauté for 10 minutes, or until the onion is translucent. Add the anchovies, garlic and thyme sprigs and cook for a further 1 minute, or until the anchovies have dissolved.

Increase the heat to high, add the veal and season with sea salt and freshly ground black pepper. Cook for 3–4 minutes, or until light golden, stirring with a wooden spoon to break up the meat. Add the mushrooms and cook for 1 minute.

Reduce the heat to medium. Add the tomato paste and cook, stirring, for 30 seconds. Pour in the wine and bring to a simmer. Cook for 4 minutes, or until the liquid has reduced by half.

Add the tomatoes, bay leaves and 125 ml (4 fl oz/½ cup) water. Bring to the boil, reduce the heat to medium–low, then cover and simmer for 30 minutes.

Remove the lid and simmer for a further 30–40 minutes, or until the ragù is thick. Remove from the heat, stir in the basil and adjust the seasoning to taste. Discard the thyme sprigs and bay leaves.

When the ragù is nearly ready, add the spaghetti to a large pot of rapidly boiling salted water and cook according to the packet instructions until al dente, about 10 minutes. Drain well.

For the next day, reserve about 375 g (13 oz/1½ cups) of the ragù for the baked stuffed eggplants. (The ragù can be refrigerated in an airtight container for up to 3 days, or frozen for up to 6 weeks.)

Divide the spaghetti among serving bowls. Spoon the ragù over the top. Scatter with shaved parmesan and extra thyme sprigs and serve.

✳ **Preparation time:** 25 minutes　✳ **Cooking time:** 1 hour 35 minutes　✳ **Serves:** 4

Beef and beer stew with carrot caraway mash

100 ml (3½ fl oz) olive oil, approximately
3 kg (6 lb 12 oz) beef osso buco
6 garlic cloves, thinly sliced
3 tablespoons chopped rosemary
10 juniper berries
1.25 litres (44 fl oz/5 cups) beer
60 g (2¼ oz/⅓ cup) soft brown sugar
80 ml (2½ fl oz/⅓ cup) balsamic vinegar

Carrot caraway mash
12 carrots, about 1.8 kg (4 lb) in total,
  sliced 2 cm (¾ inch) thick
50 g (1¾ oz) butter
3 teaspoons caraway seeds
300 g (10½ oz/2 cups) frozen peas
1 tablespoon chopped tarragon

Preheat the oven to 170°C (325°F/Gas 3).

Heat 2 tablespoons olive oil in a large flameproof casserole over medium–high heat. Season the beef and brown in three or four batches, adding more oil as needed. Transfer to a plate.

Heat another 1 tablespoon oil in the saucepan. Add the garlic, tossing constantly until it starts to turn golden, then add the rosemary and juniper berries and cook for 30 seconds. Return all the beef to the pan, with the beer, sugar and vinegar. Bring the mixture to a simmer. Cover with a sheet of baking paper, then a double layer of foil. Transfer to the oven and bake for 2 hours, or until the meat is very tender.

When the meat is nearly ready, start making the carrot caraway mash. Steam all the carrot in a large steamer over medium–high heat for 35 minutes, or until very tender. Drain well and spread on a tray for at least 10 minutes to allow the excess liquid to evaporate, then purée in a food processor. Melt the butter in a small frying pan until it turns light brown; add the caraway seeds and cook for 20 seconds, then add to the carrot purée. Season to taste with sea salt and freshly ground black pepper and keep warm.

Meanwhile, remove the beef from the sauce and keep warm. Place some kitchen paper on the surface of the sauce to absorb the excess oil, repeating as necessary. Reduce the sauce over high heat for 20–25 minutes, or until the bubbles become small and the sauce has thickened. Return the beef to the sauce.

Cook the peas in a saucepan of salted boiling water for 2 minutes, or until tender. Drain, then toss with the tarragon and a little olive oil to coat.

For the next day, reserve 80 g (2¾ oz/½ cup) of the peas, half the beef stew and half the carrot mash for the beef and beer pie. (The ingredients can be refrigerated in airtight containers for up to 3 days, but are not suitable for freezing.)

Divide the remaining carrot mash, beef stew and peas among serving plates and serve.

Beef and beer pie with carrot mash
Serves 4

Preheat the oven to 200°C (400°F/Gas 6). Break the reserved beef into chunks, remove the excess fat, then place in a 1.5 litre (52 fl oz/6 cup) baking dish with the reserved peas and gently toss. Mix the reserved carrot mash with 60 g (2¼ oz/½ cup) grated cheddar cheese, then spread over the beef and pea mixture. Bake for 30 minutes, or until heated through. Serve hot.

Greek bean stew with fried haloumi

Bean, feta and olive scone bake
Serves 6

Preheat the oven to 200°C (400°F/ Gas 6). Gently reheat the reserved bean stew in a saucepan, then cover and keep warm. Place 225 g (8 oz/1½ cups) self-raising flour in a large bowl and rub in 40 g (1½ oz) chopped butter with your fingertips until the mixture resembles breadcrumbs. Using a flat-bladed knife, stir in enough milk, yoghurt or buttermilk — about 185 ml (6 fl oz/¾ cup) — to form a soft dough. Turn the dough out onto a floured work surface and lightly knead until it just comes together (do not over-handle the dough or it will be tough). Using a rolling pin, roll the dough out to a 20 x 30 cm (8 x 12 inch) rectangle. Scatter 150 g (5½ oz/1 cup) crumbled feta and 80 g (2¾ oz/½ cup) chopped pitted kalamata olives over the top. Roll the dough up, Swiss roll (jelly roll) fashion, then cut into 12 even pieces. Spoon the hot bean stew into a large baking dish, then place the dough rounds over the surface to cover. Bake for 40 minutes, or until the scone topping is golden and crisp. Serve hot, with a green salad.

500 g (1 lb 2 oz/2½ cups) dried white beans, such as cannellini or great northern beans
80 ml (2½ fl oz/⅓ cup) extra virgin olive oil
2 large onions, chopped
3 garlic cloves, finely chopped
6 celery stalks, thinly sliced
2 large carrots, thinly sliced
2 tablespoons tomato paste (concentrated purée)
2 teaspoons ground allspice
3 dried Greek oregano sprigs, or 1 tablespoon dried oregano
500 ml (17 fl oz/2 cups) dry red wine
2 x 800 g (1 lb 12 oz) tins chopped tomatoes
90 g (3¼ oz/¼ cup) honey
2½ tablespoons red wine vinegar, or to taste
1 large handful flat-leaf (Italian) parsley, chopped, plus extra, to garnish
200 g (7 oz) haloumi, cut into wide slices 1 cm (½ inch) thick

Soak the beans in cold water overnight, then drain well. Transfer to a large saucepan, cover with cold water and bring to a simmer over medium heat. Skim off any froth that rises to the surface, then simmer for 30 minutes, or until the beans are half cooked. Drain well.

Rinse the pan and wipe dry. Heat about 2½ tablespoons of the olive oil in the pan over medium heat. Add the onion and garlic and sauté for 5–6 minutes, or until the onion has softened.

Add the celery and carrot and sauté for 6–7 minutes, or until the vegetables have softened. Add the tomato paste and allspice and cook for 1–2 minutes, then add the oregano, wine, tomatoes, honey, vinegar and beans. Mix well, then stir in just enough water to cover the beans.

Bring the mixture to a gentle simmer, then reduce the heat to low. Cover and cook, stirring occasionally, for 1 hour, or until the beans are very tender. Remove the stems of the dried oregano sprigs, if using. Stir in the parsley and season to taste with sea salt and freshly ground black pepper. Keep warm.

Heat the remaining olive oil in a large frying pan over medium heat. Fry the haloumi for 2 minutes on each side, or until light golden and heated through.

Ladle 2 spoonfuls of the bean stew into serving bowls. Top with the haloumi, sprinkle with extra parsley and serve.

For the next day, reserve the remaining bean stew for the bean, feta and olive scone bake. (The stew can be refrigerated in an airtight container for up to 3 days, or frozen for up to 3 months.)

Preparation time: 30 minutes
plus overnight soaking

Cooking time: 2 hours

Serves: 4

Preparation time: 15 minutes ✳ **Cooking time:** 1 hour 30 minutes ✳ **Serves:** 4

Mushroom, red wine and barley risotto

1 litre (35 fl oz/4 cups) chicken stock
40 g (1½ oz) butter
500 g (1 lb 2 oz) Swiss brown
  mushrooms, quartered
2 tablespoons olive oil
5 rindless bacon slices, about 300 g
  (10½ oz) in total, chopped
1 onion, finely chopped
2 garlic cloves, crushed
2 tablespoons finely chopped rosemary
300 g (10½ oz/1⅓ cups) pearl barley
125 ml (4 fl oz/½ cup) red wine
2 tablespoons torn parsley leaves
1 tablespoon crème fraiche or
  sour cream
shaved pecorino cheese, to serve

Heat the stock in a saucepan over medium heat. Keep at a low simmer.

Meanwhile, melt the butter in a large frying pan over medium–high heat. Add the mushrooms and sauté for 5–6 minutes, or until softened and light golden. Remove to a plate.

Heat the olive oil in the saucepan over medium heat. Add the bacon and onion and sauté for 5–6 minutes, or until the onion has softened and the bacon is light golden. Add the garlic and rosemary and cook for 1–2 minutes. Add the barley and stir until well coated.

Pour in the wine and continue to stir until the liquid is almost absorbed. When the wine has been absorbed, add a ladle of hot stock to the barley and continue to stir slowly until the stock has been absorbed.

Add the remaining stock, then cover and simmer for 1 hour, or until the barley is tender.

Stir in the mushrooms with any juices, along with the parsley and crème fraiche. Cook, uncovered, for 10 minutes. Season to taste with sea salt and freshly ground black pepper.

For the next day, reserve 2 cups of the risotto for the barley and parmesan patties. (The risotto can be refrigerated in an airtight container for up to 2 days, but is not suitable for freezing.)

Divide the remaining risotto among serving bowls. Scatter with shaved pecorino and serve.

Barley and parmesan patties with pear salad
Serves 4

Lightly beat 1 egg in a bowl. Add the reserved barley risotto, 50 g (1¾ oz/½ cup) grated parmesan, 50 g (1¾ oz/½ cup) dry breadcrumbs, ½ finely chopped onion and 1 small handful chopped parsley and mix well. Using floured hands, divide the mixture into 8 even-sized patties and dust lightly in flour. Heat 2 tablespoons olive oil in a frying pan and cook the patties, in batches if necessary, for 4–5 minutes on each side, or until golden, turning the patties carefully as they are quite fragile. Meanwhile, drain a 280 g (10 oz) jar of artichoke hearts, then slice and place in a bowl. Add 1 large handful rocket (arugula), 2 thinly sliced corella pears and 45 g (1½ oz/½ cup) shaved pecorino cheese. Dress with a little balsamic vinegar and extra virgin olive oil and toss to combine. Serve with the patties.

Ham and gruyère French toast

Serves 4 (makes 8)

Preheat the oven to 180ºC (350ºF/ Gas 4). Remove the meat from the reserved ham hock and thinly slice. Cut a baguette into 16 slices on the diagonal, each about 2 cm (¾ inch) thick. Butter well on one side. Top half the buttered sides with the ham and thin slices of gruyère cheese. Sandwich with the remaining slices of buttered baguette. Whisk together 2 eggs and 125 ml (4 fl oz/½ cup) milk and season with sea salt and freshly ground black pepper. Immerse each sandwich in the egg mixture and drain. Cook in a large ovenproof frying pan in plenty of butter for 2–3 minutes on each side, or until golden. Transfer the pan to the oven and bake for 5–10 minutes, or until the French toasts are firm. Serve hot.

Hearty pea and ham soup

400 g (14 oz/2 cups) dried green
   split peas
2 tablespoons olive oil
2 onions, finely chopped
3 carrots, finely chopped
3 celery stalks, finely chopped
3 thyme sprigs
2.5 litres (87 fl oz/10 cups) chicken
   stock
2 smoked ham hocks, about 1.5 kg
   (3 lb 5 oz) in total
2 bay leaves
60 ml (2 fl oz/¼ cup) cream
crusty bread, to serve

Soak the split peas in cold water overnight, then drain well and set aside.

Heat the olive oil in a large heavy-based saucepan over medium heat. Add the onion, carrot, celery and thyme sprigs and sauté for 10 minutes, or until the vegetables are tender.

Add the stock, ham hocks, bay leaves and split peas. Bring to the boil, then reduce the heat to medium–low and simmer for 1½ hours, or until the peas are very tender and the liquid has thickened.

Remove the ham hocks and set aside to cool slightly. Discard the thyme sprigs and bay leaves.

For the next day, reserve 1 ham hock for the ham and gruyère French toast. (The ham hock can be refrigerated in an airtight container for up to 3 days; without the ham, the soup can be frozen for up to 6 weeks.)

Remove the meat from the remaining hock, discarding the bones, fat and skin, and chop into small pieces.

Add the meat to the soup and allow to warm through over medium heat. Season to taste with sea salt and freshly ground black pepper, then ladle into warm serving bowls. Drizzle with the cream and serve with crusty bread.

Preparation time: 25 minutes
plus overnight soaking

Cooking time: 1 hour 45 minutes

Serves: 6

✳ **Preparation time:** 20 minutes   ✳ **Cooking time:** 1 hour 30 minutes   ✳ **Serves:** 4

Chicken, leek and bacon casserole

50 g (1¾ oz/⅓ cup) plain (all-purpose)
  flour
12 chicken drumsticks, about 2 kg
  (4 lb 8 oz) in total
80 ml (2½ fl oz/⅓ cup) olive oil,
  approximately
4 rindless bacon slices, about 150 g
  (5½ oz) in total, diced
2 leeks, white part only, rinsed well
  and thinly sliced
1 tablespoon chopped tarragon
60 ml (2 fl oz/¼ cup) white wine
250 ml (9 fl oz/1 cup) chicken stock
4 desiree potatoes, scrubbed and halved
200 g (7 oz) green beans, trimmed and
  sliced on the diagonal

Preheat the oven to 180°C (350°F/Gas 4).

Put the flour in a bowl and season with sea salt and freshly ground black pepper. Dust the chicken in the flour, shaking off the excess.

Heat 2 tablespoons of the olive oil in a large flameproof casserole dish over medium heat. Add the chicken in batches and cook for 2–3 minutes on each side, or until golden all over, adding more oil as necessary. Remove to a plate.

Add the bacon, leek and tarragon to the dish and sauté for 5–6 minutes, or until the leek has softened. Increase the heat to high and stir in the wine using a wooden spoon, scraping up any stuck-on bits from the bottom of the pan. Cook for 2–3 minutes, or until all the liquid has evaporated.

Return all the chicken to the pan with the stock. Cover, transfer to the oven and bake for 10 minutes. Place the potatoes in a baking dish, drizzle with the remaining oil and season well. Transfer to the oven and roast with the chicken for another 50 minutes, or until the chicken is cooked through and the potatoes are very tender. Season the chicken and potatoes to taste.

Just before serving time, bring a pot of water to the boil. Add the beans and cook for 2 minutes, or until tender. Drain well.

For the next day, reserve 4 drumsticks and 125 ml (4 fl oz/½ cup) of the cooking liquid for the crepes. (The ingredients can be refrigerated in airtight containers for up to 2 days, but are not suitable for freezing.)

Serve the remaining drumsticks with the beans and roast potatoes.

Baked chicken and asparagus crepes
Serves 2 as a main

Serves 4 as a light lunch

Preheat the oven to 180°C (350°F/Gas 4). Remove the meat from the reserved chicken drumsticks and finely chop or shred. Place in a small saucepan with the reserved cooking liquid and cook over medium heat for 4–5 minutes, or until the liquid has reduced and thickened. Remove from the heat and stir in 2 tablespoons sour cream and 1 tablespoon chopped parsley. Lay four 18 cm (7 inch) ready-made crepes on a work surface, then place the chicken mixture down the centre of each. Blanch 4 asparagus spears and place 1 spear on each crepe. Roll the crepes up and lay them neatly in a buttered 21 x 16 cm (8¼ x 6¼ inch) baking dish. Scatter 65 g (2¼ oz/½ cup) grated gruyère cheese over and bake for 10–15 minutes, or until golden. Serve with a green salad.

Spanish sausage rolls

Serves 4

Preheat the oven to 210°C (415°F/ Gas 6–7). Strip the meat from the reserved lamb shanks and chop, removing the excess fat and sinew. Place in a bowl with the reserved chorizo mixture and the reserved rice. Take three 25 cm (10 inch) square sheets of thawed frozen puff pastry and cut each in half. Moisten one long edge of each rectangle with water. Place 125 g (4½ oz/⅔ cup) of the shank mixture on the other long edge, leaving 2 cm (¾ inch) free at each end. Roll towards the moistened edge, placing the seam underneath, then seal the ends with a fork. Repeat with the remaining pastry and filling. Place on baking trays and bake for 30–40 minutes, or until the pastry is golden and crisp. Cut each log into 4 or 5 pieces on the diagonal. Serve with a green salad and good tomato chutney.

Lamb shanks with chorizo, mushrooms and buttered rice

60 ml (2 fl oz/¼ cup) extra virgin olive oil
8 French-trimmed lamb shanks, about 400 g (14 oz) each
2 onions, chopped
2 chorizo sausages, quartered lengthways and sliced into 1 cm (½ inch) pieces
300 g (10½ oz) Swiss brown mushrooms, cut into 2 cm (¾ inch) wedges
2 garlic cloves, thinly sliced
250 ml (9 fl oz/1 cup) good sweet sherry
750 ml (26 fl oz/3 cups) chicken stock
thyme sprigs, to garnish

Buttered rice
400 g (14 oz/2 cups) long-grain white rice
3 teaspoons thyme
30 g (1 oz) butter, chopped
90 g (3¼ oz/1 cup) flaked almonds, toasted

Preheat the oven to 160°C (315°F/Gas 2–3).

Heat 1 tablespoon of the olive oil in a large flameproof casserole dish over medium–high heat. Season the shanks well with sea salt and freshly ground black pepper. Add to the pan and brown in several batches, turning every couple of minutes. Remove to a plate.

Heat the remaining oil in the dish over medium–low heat. Add the onion, sausage, mushrooms and garlic and sauté for 15 minutes, or until the onion is very soft and translucent.

Pour in the sherry, increase the heat to high and boil for 5 minutes. Add the stock and the lamb shanks and bring to a simmer. Lay a sheet of baking paper over the surface, then cover with a lid or foil. Transfer to the oven and bake for 2½ hours, or until the shanks are very tender.

Meanwhile, make the buttered rice. Put the rice and 625 ml (21½ fl oz/2½ cups) cold water in a saucepan, stir well and bring to the boil over high heat. Cover, reduce the heat to low and cook for 12 minutes, or until the rice is tender and the liquid has been absorbed. Remove from the heat, then stand, covered, for 10 minutes, or up to 90 minutes. Add the remaining buttered rice ingredients and fluff with a fork.

Remove the shanks from the cooking liquid. Place some kitchen paper on the surface of the sauce to absorb any excess oil, repeating as necessary. Place back over high heat and cook for 15 minutes, or until the sauce has reduced by half.

For the next day, reserve 4 lamb shanks, 1 cup of the mushroom and chorizo mixture and one-third of the rice for the Spanish sausage rolls. (The ingredients can be refrigerated in airtight containers for up to 2 days, but are not suitable for freezing.)

Serve the remaining shanks and sauce with the remaining rice, garnished with thyme sprigs.

✳ Preparation time: 30 minutes **✳ Cooking time:** 3 hours 20 minutes **✳ Serves:** 4

Preparation time: 20 minutes   **Cooking time:** 1 hour 40 minutes   **Serves:** 4

Corned beef with braised cabbage

1.5 kg (3 lb 5 oz) piece of corned beef
60 ml (2 fl oz/¼ cup) malt vinegar
2 tablespoons olive oil
3 large onions, thinly sliced
60 g (2¼ oz/¼ cup) wholegrain mustard
1 tablespoon honey
125 ml (4 fl oz/½ cup) chicken stock
¼ large cabbage, about 500 g (1 lb 2 oz)
  in total, shredded
1 kg (2 lb 4 oz) floury potatoes, such as
  sebago, peeled and chopped
40 g (1½ oz) butter
200 ml (7 fl oz) milk
finely chopped flat-leaf (Italian) parsley,
  to serve
tomato chutney, to serve

Place the beef in a large saucepan. Add 2 tablespoons of the vinegar and enough water to just cover the beef. Bring to the boil, then reduce the heat to a gentle simmer. Cover and cook over low heat for 1½ hours. Remove the beef from the cooking liquid, draining well, then transfer to a warmed plate and cover with foil to keep warm.

Meanwhile, heat the olive oil in a large frying pan over medium heat. Add the onion and sauté for 12–15 minutes, or until the onion is softened and browned. Add the remaining vinegar. Bring to a simmer, then cook for 5 minutes, or until the onion has caramelised. Add the mustard, honey, stock and cabbage and stir well. Cover and cook, stirring occasionally, for 5 minutes, or until the cabbage is tender. Season to taste with sea salt and freshly ground black pepper. Keep warm.

Meanwhile, cook the potato in a large saucepan of salted boiling water for 15 minutes, or until tender. Drain well, then return to the pan with the butter and milk and mash until smooth. Keep warm.

For the next day, reserve 300 g (10½ oz) of the corned beef, 200 g (7 oz/1 cup) of the cabbage mixture and 230 g (8 oz/1 cup) of the mashed potato for the bubble and squeak fritters. (The ingredients can be refrigerated in airtight containers for up to 2 days, but are not suitable for freezing.)

Thinly slice the remaining corned beef and arrange on serving plates with the remaining braised cabbage and mashed potato. Sprinkle with parsley and serve with tomato chutney.

Bubble and squeak fritters
Serves 4

Preheat the oven to 180°C (350°F/Gas 4). Finely chop the reserved corned beef and place in a bowl with the reserved mashed potato and braised cabbage. Season to taste with sea salt and freshly ground black pepper, mix well, then shape into 12 patties. Lightly beat 2 eggs in a bowl. Place 100 g (3½ oz/2 cups) panko (Japanese breadcrumbs) in a separate bowl. Coat the patties in the egg, then the breadcrumbs. Place on a greased baking tray in a single layer and brush with olive oil. Bake for 30 minutes, or until golden, turning after 15 minutes. Serve with steamed green vegetables and tomato chutney.

Potato, tuna and leek gratin

Serves 4

Preheat the oven to 180°C (350°F/ Gas 4). Melt 60 g (2¼ oz) unsalted butter in a large non-stick frying pan over medium heat. Add 2 finely chopped leeks, white part only, and sauté for 10 minutes, or until very soft. Add 1 thinly sliced fennel bulb and cook for 5 minutes, or until soft; place in a bowl to cool. Add a 185 g (6½ oz) tin of drained flaked tuna, 1½ tablespoons chopped dill and 1 tablespoon finely grated lemon rind; m̶   ̶   ̶ ̶side. Thinly slice̶   ̶   ̶   ̶s and arrang̶   ̶   ̶   ̶sed baking d̶   ̶   ̶   ̶r of the tuna, ̶   ̶   ̶   ̶ture. Repeat in ̶   ̶   ̶ ̶ing potato, and t̶   ̶   ̶ fennel and leek̶   ̶   ̶ pour 400 ml (14 ̶   ̶ over the top, then sprin̶   ̶ 30 g (1 oz/¼ cup) grated cheese. Bake for 40 minu̶   ̶ or until golden. Set aside for 10 minutes to rest, then serve with a green salad.

Lamb chops with crushed potatoes, capers and feta

8 large lamb loin chops
80 ml (2½ fl oz/⅓ cup) lemon juice
1½ teaspoons dried oregano
2 garlic cloves, crushed
125 ml (4 fl oz/½ cup) olive oil
2 kg (4 lb 8 oz) desiree potatoes, peeled and cut into 4 cm (1½ inch) chunks
2½ tablespoons capers
150 g (5½ oz/1 cup) crumbled feta cheese
1 tablespoon finely grated lemon rind
1 small handful flat-leaf (Italian) parsley, chopped
tapenade, to serve

Preheat the oven to 200°C (400°F/Gas 6).

Place the lamb chops in a ceramic, glass or stainless steel dish. In a small bowl, mix together the lemon juice, oregano, garlic and 2 tablespoons of the olive oil. Pour over the lamb and set aside for 20 minutes to marinate.

Meanwhile, place the potatoes in a large saucepan of salted cold water. Bring to the boil and cook for 15 minutes, or until tender. Drain well.

For the next day, reserve half the potatoes for the potato, tuna and leek gratin. (The potatoes can be refrigerated in an airtight container for up to 2 days, but are not suitable for freezing.)

Place the remaining potatoes in a baking dish and scatter the capers, feta and lemon rind over the top. Drizzle with the remaining olive oil and season with freshly ground black pepper. Roast for 15 minutes, or until golden. Using a potato masher, coarsely crush the potatoes.

Meanwhile, heat a chargrill pan or barbecue hotplate to medium. Add the lamb chops and cook for 3 minutes on each side, or until done to your liking.

Divide the potatoes among serving plates and sprinkle the parsley over. Arrange the lamb chops over the top and serve with tapenade.

Preparation time: 10 minutes
plus 20 minutes marinating

Cooking time: 35 minutes

Serves: 4

Preparation time: 10 minutes   **Cooking time:** 35 minutes   **Serves:** 4

Sausages with polenta and broccoli

1 tablespoon vegetable oil
12 Italian sausages, about 1.25 kg
  (2 lb 12 oz) in total
400 g (14 oz) fennel bulb, thinly sliced
1 onion, thinly sliced
250 ml (9 fl oz /1 cup) beef stock
1 litre (35 fl oz/4 cups) chicken stock
1 litre (35 fl oz/4 cups) milk
300 g (10½ oz/2 cups) polenta
500 g (1 lb 2 oz) broccoli, cut into florets
100 g (3½ oz/1 cup) grated pecorino
  cheese
400 g (14 oz) tin borlotti beans, rinsed
  and drained

Preheat the oven to 180°C (350°F/Gas 4).

Heat the oil in a large flameproof casserole dish over medium heat. Add the sausages and cook, turning often, for 5 minutes, or until browned all over. Remove to a plate.

Add the fennel and onion to the dish and sauté for 10 minutes, or until caramelised and golden. Return the sausages to the dish and pour in the beef stock. Transfer to the oven and bake for 15 minutes, or until the sausages are cooked through.

Meanwhile, combine the chicken stock and milk in a saucepan and heat until simmering. Stirring constantly to prevent lumps forming, slowly pour in the polenta and bring to a simmer over medium heat. Reduce the heat to low and cook, stirring, for 10–15 minutes, or until the polenta is nearly tender. Remove from the heat, cover and leave to stand for 5 minutes.

Meanwhile, bring another pan of water to the boil. Add the broccoli and blanch for 4 minutes, or until just tender. Drain well and keep warm.

For the next day, remove 4 sausages from the casserole and slice into rounds. Drain the broccoli and refresh half by rinsing it under cold running water. Working quickly, stir the pecorino into the polenta, then remove half the polenta mixture to a bowl. Stir in the sliced sausages, blanched broccoli and the borlotti beans. Pour into a greased 25 x 30 cm (10 x 12 inch) baking dish. Allow to cool, then cover and refrigerate. Also reserve 1 cup of the fennel sauce for the golden fried polenta. (The polenta and fennel sauce can be refrigerated in airtight containers for up to 2 days, but are not suitable for freezing.)

Reheat the remaining sausage and fennel mixture on the stovetop over medium heat for about 5 minutes, skimming any excess fat from the surface. Serve the remaining hot polenta with the remaining broccoli, topped with the remaining sausage and fennel mixture.

Golden fried polenta with borlotti beans
Serves 6

Turn the reserved polenta mixture out onto a chopping board and cut into 12 even portions. Dust each piece in polenta. Heat 125 ml (4 fl oz/½ cup) vegetable oil in a frying pan over medium heat. Add the polenta pieces and fry for 2 minutes on each side, or until light golden. Reheat the reserved fennel sauce and serve over the polenta, sprinkled with 1 tablespoon chopped parsley and some grated pecorino cheese.

Ligurian mashed potato pie

Serves 4–6

Put the reserved mashed potato mixture into a bowl; crumble the reserved pancetta over the top. In a frying pan, heat 2 tablespoons olive oil over low heat. Finely slice the reserved beans, then add to the pan with 1 chopped onion and sauté for 10–12 minutes, or until the onion is soft. Add to the potato and pancetta mixture with 125 g (4½ oz/½ cup) firm fresh ricotta cheese, 75 g (2½ oz/¾ cup) grated parmesan and 3 lightly beaten eggs, then mix together. Grease a shallow 1.5 litre (52 fl oz/6 cup) ceramic baking dish with olive oil; sprinkle with fine fresh breadcrumbs, shake them around to coat, then tip out the excess crumbs. Spoon the potato mixture into the dish, smoothing the surface, then top with another 40 g (1½ oz/½ cup) fresh breadcrumbs. Drizzle with olive oil and bake for 40 minutes, or until golden. Serve with a green salad.

Fish with olive oil mash and crisp pancetta

1.8 kg (4 lb) desiree potatoes, or floury potatoes, peeled and chopped
125 ml (4 fl oz/½ cup) extra virgin olive oil
3 garlic cloves, thinly sliced
1 tablespoon marjoram, plus extra small leaves, to garnish
6 thin pancetta slices, about 100 g (3½ oz) in total
4 x 180 g (6 oz) blue eye trevalla fillets, or other firm white fish fillets
400 g (14 oz) green beans, trimmed
50 g (1¾ oz/½ cup) shaved parmesan
lemon cheeks, to serve

Bring a saucepan of salted water to the boil. Add the potatoes and cook for 13–15 minutes, or until very tender. Drain well, then return to the pan. Cook over low heat for 2–3 minutes to dry the potatoes, shaking the pan occasionally.

When the potatoes are nearly cooked, heat 80 ml (2½ fl oz/⅓ cup) of the olive oil in a frying pan over low heat. Add the garlic and fry gently for 2–3 minutes, or until starting to turn golden. Add the marjoram and cook for a further 20 seconds.

Mash the potatoes while they are still hot, then add the garlic oil mixture to the mash and fold through. Cover to keep warm.

Meanwhile, preheat the grill (broiler) to high. Lay the pancetta on a baking tray and grill (broil) for 2–3 minutes, or until just crisp.

Season the fish fillets with sea salt and freshly ground black pepper. Heat the remaining oil in a large frying pan over high heat. Add the fish, then cover and cook for 2–3 minutes on each side, or until golden and just cooked through.

Meanwhile, blanch the beans in a saucepan of boiling water for 2 minutes, then refresh under cold running water. Drain well.

For the next day, reserve half the mash, pancetta and beans for the Ligurian potato and bean pie. (The ingredients can be refrigerated in airtight containers for up to 2 days, but are not suitable for freezing.)

Mix the parmesan through the remaining mash, then spoon onto serving plates. Top each with a fish fillet. Crumble the pancetta over the top, scatter with small marjoram leaves and serve with the beans and lemon cheeks.

Preparation time: 30 minutes   Cooking time: 25 minutes   Serves: 4

Preparation time: 20 minutes
plus 30 minutes soaking

Cooking time: 1 hour 10 minutes

Serves: 4

Saffron chicken with green olives and sweet potato

a pinch of saffron threads
375 ml (13 fl oz/1½ cups) hot
   chicken stock
80 ml (2½ fl oz/⅓ cup) olive oil
10 chicken thigh fillets, about 1.5 kg
   (3 lb 5 oz) in total, trimmed of excess
   fat, then cut into thirds
2 onions, finely diced
2 garlic cloves, chopped
80 ml (2½ fl oz/⅓ cup) sherry vinegar
2 bay leaves
75 g (2½ oz/⅓ cup) chopped pitted
   green olives
40 g (1½ oz/¼ cup) chopped raisins
1 large sweet potato, about 600 g
   (1 lb 5 oz), peeled and cut into
   2 cm (¾ inch) chunks
steamed white rice, to serve

Feta-yoghurt cream

160 g (5¾ oz/⅔ cup) Greek yoghurt
60 g (2¼ oz/¼ cup) crumbled
   feta cheese
2 tablespoons extra virgin olive oil

In a small bowl, soak the saffron in the stock for 30 minutes.

Combine the feta-yoghurt cream ingredients in a small food processor. Blend until smooth and well combined, then season to taste with sea salt and freshly ground black pepper. Transfer to a bowl, cover and refrigerate until required.

Heat 2 tablespoons of the olive oil in a large frying pan over medium–high heat. Add the chicken in batches and fry for 6–8 minutes, or until browned all over, turning often. Remove the chicken to a bowl.

Reduce the heat to medium–low. Heat the remaining oil in the pan, then add the onion and sauté for 6–7 minutes, or until softened and golden.

Return all the chicken to the pan. Stir in the garlic, saffron stock, stock, vinegar, bay leaves, olives and raisins. Bring to the boil, adding a little water or extra stock if needed to just cover the chicken. Reduce the heat to low, then cover and simmer for 20 minutes.

Add the sweet potato and cook for a further 20–25 minutes, or until the chicken and sweet potato are cooked through. Season to taste.

For the next day, drain off about 2 cups of the chicken mixture and reserve for the empanadas. (The chicken mixture can be refrigerated in an airtight container for up to 2 days, but is not suitable for freezing.)

Serve the remaining chicken mixture with steamed rice, with the feta-yoghurt cream on the side for spooning over.

Chicken empanadas
Makes 16

Preheat the oven to 200°C (400°F/ Gas 6). Thaw 4 sheets of frozen puff pastry, then cut four 12 cm (4½ inch) circles from each sheet. Chop the reserved, drained chicken mixture into small pieces and place 1½ tablespoons of the mixture in the middle of each pastry circle. Moisten the pastry edges lightly with water, then fold the pastry circles over to form semi-circles and enclose the filling. Press the edges together with a fork to seal. Prick the top of each empanada with a fork to allow the steam to escape. Place on a baking tray and bake for 15–20 minutes, or until golden brown. Serve warm or at room temperature.

Pork patties with corn salsa

Serves 4

Remove the kernels from 2 corn cobs. Peel and cut 500 g (1 lb 2 oz) potatoes into 1 cm (½ inch) dice. Heat a large, lightly oiled frying pan over medium heat. Add the corn, potato and 1 chopped red capsicum (pepper) and sauté for 10 minutes, or until the potato is tender. Add 4 chopped tomatoes and 125 ml (4 fl oz/½ cup) water and bring to the boil. Reduce the heat to low, then cover and simmer for 10 minutes, or until the liquid has evaporated. Stir in 1 tablespoon sweet chilli sauce and cook for 1 minute. Meanwhile, shred the reserved pork and place in a large bowl. Add 500 g (1 lb 2 oz) minced (ground) pork, 1 lightly beaten egg, 85 g (3 oz/⅔ cup) mild grated cheddar cheese, 2 crushed garlic cloves and 1 finely chopped long red chilli. Season with sea salt and freshly ground black pepper and mix together well. Shape into 8 patties, using about 90 g (3¼ oz/½ cup) of mixture per patty. Cook the patties in a large, lightly oiled frying pan over medium heat for 5 minutes on each side, or until lightly browned and cooked through. Serve with the warm corn salsa, soft tortillas and spoonfuls of guacamole.

Tex-Mex bollito misto

2 tablespoons olive oil
1.5 kg (3 lb 5 oz) pork neck, trimmed
2 large red capsicums (peppers), chopped
1 large green capsicum (pepper), chopped
2 small green chillies, chopped
1 tablespoon smoked paprika
2 teaspoons ground coriander
2 teaspoons ground cumin
1 litre (35 fl oz/4 cups) chicken stock
400 g (14 oz) tin chopped tomatoes
2 x 400 g (14 oz) tins butterbeans (lima beans), rinsed and drained
2 vine-ripened tomatoes, finely chopped
1 large handful flat-leaf (Italian) parsley, chopped
lime wedges, to serve

Heat the olive oil in a large flameproof casserole dish over medium heat. Add the pork neck and cook for 5 minutes, or until browned all over, turning often. Remove to a plate.

Add the capsicums and chilli to the dish and sauté for 5 minutes, or until the capsicum has softened. Add the spices and cook, stirring, for 1 minute, or until fragrant.

Return the pork to the pan with the stock, tinned tomatoes and 250 ml (9 fl oz/1 cup) water. Bring to a simmer, then reduce the heat to low. Cover and cook for 1 hour, or until the pork is tender.

Stir in the beans, fresh tomatoes and parsley and cook for 5 minutes to heat through.

For the next day, remove the pork from the casserole, then cut off and reserve one-third of the pork for the patties. (The pork can be refrigerated in an airtight container for up to 2 days, but is not suitable for freezing.)

Carve the remaining pork into slices 1 cm (½ inch) thick. Divide among shallow serving bowls, ladle the bean mixture over and serve with lime wedges.

✳ **Preparation time:** 20 minutes ✳ **Cooking time:** 1 hour 20 minutes ✳ **Serves:** 4

Preparation time: 20 minutes   ✳   **Cooking time:** 20 minutes   ✳   **Serves:** 4

Roast chicken tenderloins in pancetta with cauliflower purée

12 chicken tenderloins, about 750 g
  (1 lb 10 oz) in total, or 4 chicken breast
  fillets, each sliced on the diagonal into
  three even lengths
12 large basil leaves
12 thin slices of mild pancetta, about
  200 g (7 oz) in total
olive oil, for brushing
2 large cauliflowers, about 1.4 kg
  (3 lb 2 oz) in total, cut into florets
25 g (1 oz/¼ cup) grated parmesan
60 g (2¼ oz/¼ cup) crème fraiche
  or sour cream
½ teaspoon thyme or finely snipped
  chives
¼ teaspoon grated orange rind (optional)
lemon wedges, to serve
green leaf salad, to serve

Preheat the oven to 190°C (375°F/Gas 5).

Season the chicken with sea salt and freshly ground black pepper. Lay a basil leaf over the top of each piece, then wrap a pancetta slice around each one, tucking the edges underneath the chicken to enclose it. Brush the pancetta lightly with oil, then transfer to a lightly oiled roasting tin and roast for 17–18 minutes, or until the pancetta is crisp and the chicken is cooked through.

Meanwhile, working in batches if necessary, place the cauliflower florets in a steamer basket set over a large saucepan of boiling water. Cover and cook for 4 minutes, or until tender.

For the next day, reserve half the cauliflower florets for the spicy cauliflower with tomato sauce. (The cauliflower can be refrigerated in an airtight container for up to 3 days, but is not suitable for freezing.)

Transfer the remaining cauliflower to a food processor with the parmesan, crème fraiche, thyme and orange rind, if using. Blend until smooth, then season to taste.

Arrange three chicken tenderloins on each serving plate and spoon the cauliflower purée alongside. Serve with lemon wedges and a green leaf salad.

Spicy cauliflower with tomato sauce
Serves 4

Heat 60 ml (2 fl oz/¼ cup) vegetable oil in a large saucepan over medium heat. Add ½ teaspoon brown mustard seeds, 1 chopped onion and 1 chopped garlic clove. Sauté for 3 minutes, or until the seeds start to pop. Stir in ½ teaspoon ground turmeric, 1 teaspoon chopped fresh ginger, ¼ teaspoon cayenne pepper and ½ teaspoon garam masala. Cook, stirring, for 2 minutes, or until fragrant. Add 3 chopped tomatoes and 1 chopped red chilli and simmer for 20 minutes, or until thickened. Stir in 1 tablespoon chopped coriander (cilantro) and set aside. In a bowl, combine 200 g (7 oz/1½ cups) besan (chickpea flour), 1 teaspoon baking powder, ½ teaspoon ground turmeric, 2 tablespoons chopped coriander (cilantro) and 1 teaspoon sea salt. Whisk in 330 ml (11¼ fl oz/1⅓ cups) water, or enough to form a batter, then stir in 2 tablespoons peanut oil. Heat enough oil for deep-frying in a large saucepan or wok over medium heat. In batches, dip the reserved cauliflower florets in the batter, allowing the excess to drain off. Deep-fry for 3–4 minutes, or until golden and crisp. Drain well and serve with the tomato sauce, mango chutney, lime pickles, plain yoghurt and naan bread.

Meatloaf bake with onions and cream
Serves 4

Preheat the oven to 190°C (375°F/Gas 5). Bring the reserved meatloaf and balsamic onion sauce to room temperature. Cut the meatloaf into slices and arrange in a generously buttered shallow baking dish. Spread the balsamic onion sauce over the meatloaf, then drizzle with 250 ml (9 fl oz/1 cup) cream and crumble 50 g (1¾ oz) blue cheese over the top. Peel and very thinly slice 2 potatoes, then arrange them neatly over the top of the cheese to cover all the ingredients. Cover with foil and bake for 35–40 minutes, or until the potato is tender. Remove the foil and bake for a further 10–15 minutes, or until the potato is golden. Serve hot.

Pork and prune meatloaf with balsamic onion sauce

1.25 kg (2 lb 12 oz) minced (ground) pork, not too lean
1 onion, finely chopped
2 garlic cloves, crushed
1 tablespoon dijon mustard
160 g (5¾ oz/2 cups) fresh breadcrumbs
1 small handful flat-leaf (Italian) parsley, chopped
1 tablespoon chopped sage
2 eggs, lightly beaten
80 ml (2½ fl oz/⅓ cup) tomato passata (puréed tomatoes)
60 ml (2 fl oz/¼ cup) red wine
8 rindless bacon slices, about 200 g (7 oz) in total
220 g (7¾ oz/1 cup) pitted prunes, chopped

Balsamic onion sauce
25 g (1 oz) unsalted butter
2½ tablespoons olive oil
6 onions, sliced into rings
1 teaspoon thyme leaves
125 ml (4 fl oz/½ cup) balsamic vinegar
250 ml (9 fl oz/1 cup) chicken or veal stock
2½ tablespoons soft brown sugar

Preheat the oven to 180°C (350°F/Gas 4). Line a large baking tray with baking paper.

Combine the pork, onion, garlic, mustard, breadcrumbs, parsley and sage in a large bowl. Season with sea salt and freshly ground black pepper. Add the eggs, passata and wine and mix well using your hands.

Turn the mixture out onto a sheet of baking paper. Keeping it on the paper, spread it into a 25 x 35 cm (10 x 14 inch) rectangle. Arrange the bacon slices, slightly overlapping each other, side by side lengthways over the top. Scatter the prunes over the bacon.

Starting from a narrow end, roll the meat up like a Swiss roll (jelly roll), using the paper as a guide, peeling back the paper as you roll. Transfer the meatloaf onto the baking tray, seam side down. Bake for 1 hour, or until cooked through and browned. Remove from the oven and set aside for 15 minutes before slicing.

While the meatloaf is baking, make the balsamic onion sauce. Heat the butter and olive oil in a large heavy-based saucepan over medium–low heat. Add the onion and cook for 15 minutes, or until lightly golden, stirring occasionally. Stir in the thyme and vinegar and cook for 1 minute. Add the stock and sugar and bring to a simmer. Reduce the heat to low, then cover the mixture with a crushed piece of baking paper and a lid. Cook slowly for 30 minutes, stirring occasionally to stop the mixture sticking to the pan. Remove the lid and cook for a further 5–10 minutes, if necessary, until the sauce is thick and syrupy. Season to taste.

For the next day, reserve half the meatloaf and half the balsamic onion sauce for the meatloaf bake. (The ingredients can be refrigerated in airtight containers for up to 5 days, but are not suitable for freezing.)

Cut the remaining meatloaf into thick slices and serve with the remaining balsamic onion sauce.

Preparation time: 30 minutes　　**Cooking time:** 1 hour　　**Serves:** 4

Preparation time: 20 minutes **Cooking time:** 15 minutes **Serves:** 4

Chinese pork noodles

80 ml (2½ fl oz/⅓ cup) Chinese yellow
 bean sauce (available from large
 supermarkets and Asian food stores)
80 ml (2½ fl oz/⅓ cup) hoisin sauce
2 tablespoons soy sauce
2 tablespoons Chinese rice wine
2 tablespoons soft brown sugar
2 teaspoons sesame oil
60 ml (2 fl oz/¼ cup) peanut oil
2 onions, thinly sliced
5 garlic cloves, finely chopped
1 kg (2 lb 4 oz) minced (ground) pork
400 g (14 oz) fresh egg noodles
1 small cucumber, cut into fine
 matchsticks
2 spring onions (scallions), cut into
 curls or fine matchsticks
chopped roasted peanuts, to serve

Combine the yellow bean, hoisin and soy sauce
in a bowl with the rice wine, sugar, sesame oil
and 80 ml (2½ fl oz/⅓ cup) water. Mix well to
dissolve the sugar, then set aside.

Heat a wok over high heat. Add about
1½ tablespoons of the peanut oil, then add the
onion and garlic and stir-fry for 4–5 minutes, or
until golden. Remove to a plate.

Add the pork to the wok in batches for
2–3 minutes each time, stirring constantly to
break up any lumps, and adding more oil as
needed. Remove each batch to a bowl.

Return the onion mixture and all the pork
to the wok. Add the hoisin sauce mixture and
stir-fry for a further 3 minutes, or until the liquid
has reduced a little.

Meanwhile, cook the noodles in a large pot of
boiling water until just soft, following the packet
instructions. Drain well.

For the next day, reserve half the pork mixture
for the tofu-pork with sichuan pepper. (The
pork mixture can be refrigerated in an airtight
container for up to 3 days, but is not suitable
for freezing.)

Toss the remaining pork mixture through the
noodles. Serve garnished with the cucumber,
spring onion and peanuts.

Tofu-pork with sichuan pepper
Serves 4–6

Heat a wok over medium heat.
Add the reserved pork mixture,
60 ml (2 fl oz/¼ cup) water and
2–3 tablespoons Chinese chilli
paste (or to taste). Cook, stirring
now and then, for 5 minutes, or
until heated through. Cut two
300 g (10½ oz) blocks of drained
firm silken tofu into 2 cm (¾ inch)
dice. Add the tofu to the warmed
pork mixture and very gently toss
using a large spatula. In a small
bowl, combine 1 teaspoon ground
sichuan peppercorns, ½ teaspoon
crushed sea salt and ¼ teaspoon
crushed white pepper. Serve the
tofu and pork mixture on beds of
steamed rice, sprinkled with the
sichuan pepper mixture and thinly
sliced spring onions (scallions).

Chicken biryani

Serves 4

Remove the meat from the reserved chicken tandoori pieces, then shred. Combine in a bowl with 85 g (3 oz/⅔ cup) sultanas (golden raisins). Heat 2 tablespoons vegetable oil and 40 g (1½ oz) butter in a large frying pan over medium–high heat. Add 2 large thinly sliced onions and cook for 20 minutes, or until browned lightly, stirring occasionally. Add 1 crushed garlic clove, 2 teaspoons garam masala, 4 bruised cardamom pods, 1 cinnamon stick and 400 g (14 oz/2 cups) basmati rice. Cook, stirring, for 1 minute, or until the rice is coated in the spices. Add 500 ml (17 fl oz/2 cups) chicken stock and 250 ml (9 fl oz/ 1 cup) water and bring to the boil. Reduce the heat, cover and simmer over low heat for 2 minutes. Add 300 g (10½ oz) trimmed green beans, then cover and cook for another 10 minutes, or until the rice is cooked through and the beans are tender. Discard the cardamom pods and cinnamon stick. Stir in the shredded chicken mixture and cook for 5 minutes, or until heated through. Serve sprinkled with chopped coriander (cilantro) leaves and 45 g (1½ oz/½ cup) roasted slivered almonds, with lemon wedges for squeezing over.

Tandoori roast chicken

2 x 1.4 kg (3 lb 2 oz) chickens,
 each cut into 8 pieces
2 Lebanese (short) cucumbers,
 cut lengthways and seeded
150 g (5½ oz) Greek yoghurt
1 small red onion, thinly sliced
2 vine-ripened tomatoes, chopped
1 small handful coriander (cilantro)
 leaves
1 tablespoon lemon juice
naan bread, to serve
lemon wedges, to serve

Tandoori marinade

1 onion, grated
2 teaspoons ground coriander
2 teaspoons finely grated fresh ginger
2 teaspoons finely grated lemon rind
1 tablespoon lemon juice
60 g (2¼ oz/¼ cup) tandoori paste
1 teaspoon sea salt
150 g (5½ oz) Greek yoghurt

In a large ceramic, glass or non-metallic bowl, combine the tandoori marinade ingredients and mix together well. Using a small sharp knife, cut several deep diagonal slits into each piece of chicken. Add the chicken to the marinade and toss to coat, rubbing it in well. Cover and marinate in the refrigerator for at least 4 hours, or overnight.

Preheat the oven to 220°C (425°C/Gas 7). Drain the chicken well, discarding the marinade. Arrange the chicken in a single layer on a greased wire rack set over a baking tray. Transfer to the oven and roast for 40 minutes, or until the chicken is cooked through.

Meanwhile, roughly grate one of the cucumbers, then use your hands to squeeze out the excess liquid. Combine the grated cucumber in a small bowl with the yoghurt. Mix well and set aside.

Chop the remaining cucumber and combine in another bowl with the onion, tomato, coriander and lemon juice.

For the next day, reserve half the tandoori chicken for the chicken biryani. (The tandoori chicken can be refrigerated in an airtight container for up to 2 days, but is not suitable for freezing.)

Serve the remaining tandoori chicken with the tomato salad, cucumber-yoghurt sauce, naan bread and lemon wedges.

Preparation time: 20 minutes
plus at least 4 hours marinating

Cooking time: 40 minutes

Serves: 4

Preparation time: 20 minutes　　**Cooking time:** 45 minutes　　**Serves:** 4

Silverbeet, chickpea and almond tagine

2 tablespoons olive oil

2 red onions, thinly sliced

2 garlic cloves, crushed

2 teaspoons ground cumin

1½ teaspoons ground cinnamon

½ teaspoon chilli powder

350 g (12 oz) butternut pumpkin (squash), peeled, seeded and cut into 2 cm (¾ inch) wedges

2 x 400 g (14 oz) tins chopped tomatoes

400 g (14 oz) tin chickpeas, rinsed and drained

1 small cauliflower, cut into florets

1 kg (2 lb 4 oz/1 bunch) silverbeet (Swiss chard), washed, stems trimmed and chopped

1 tablespoon finely chopped preserved lemon rind, or 2 teaspoons finely grated lemon rind

couscous, to serve

1 handful coriander (cilantro) leaves

50 g (1¾ oz/⅓ cup) whole roasted almonds, roughly chopped

lemon wedges, to serve

Heat the olive oil in a large heavy-based saucepan over medium heat. Add the onion and sauté for 7–10 minutes, or until translucent. Add the garlic and spices and cook for a further 30 seconds, or until fragrant.

Add the pumpkin, tomatoes, chickpeas and 250 ml (9 fl oz/1 cup) water. Cover, bring to the boil, then reduce the heat to medium–low and cook for 20 minutes, stirring occasionally.

Add the cauliflower and cook for a further 10 minutes, or until the vegetables are tender.

Stir in the silverbeet and preserved lemon and simmer gently for 3 minutes. Season to taste with sea salt and freshly ground black pepper.

For the next day, drain off about 2 cups of the tagine and reserve for the Moroccan filo pastries. (The tagine can be refrigerated in an airtight container for up to 3 days, or frozen for up to 1 month.)

Spoon the tagine into serving bowls and sprinkle with the coriander and almonds. Serve with couscous and lemon wedges.

Moroccan filo pastries
Makes about 36

Preheat the oven to 190°C (375°F/ Gas 5). Drain any excess liquid from the reserved tagine mixture — if it is too wet, the pastries will be soggy. Add 2 tablespoons chopped coriander (cilantro), 2 tablespoons chopped roasted almonds and 75 g (2½ oz/½ cup) crumbled feta. Break up any large chunks of vegetables with a fork. Cut 9 filo pastry sheets into 4 long strips each and cover with a damp tea towel (dish towel) so the pastry doesn't dry out. Working in batches, brush each pastry strip with butter. Spoon 1 heaped teaspoonful of the mixture into the bottom corner, leaving a small border. Fold the pastry over the filling to form a triangle; continue folding until the triangle is sealed. Place on a baking tray covered with baking paper and repeat with the remaining pastry and filling. Brush generously with melted butter and bake for 10–12 minutes, or until golden. (These pastries also freeze well before they are cooked.) Serve with a spicy chutney or minted yoghurt dip.

Snapper pilaff rolls

Serves 4

Blanch 8 large savoy cabbage leaves in a saucepan of salted boiling water for 1–2 minutes, or until softened. Drain well, then refresh in iced water and drain again. Remove the hard core from the blanched leaves, then cut each leaf into a rough rectangle, measuring about 16 x 22 cm (6¼ x 8½ inches). Flake the reserved fish into 2 cm (¾ inch) chunks and mix with the reserved pilaff. Place about 60 g (2¼ oz/ ⅓ cup) of the mixture along the short edge of a cabbage leaf. Fold the closest end over the mixture, fold the sides in, then roll, placing the seam underneath to secure. Place in a steamer and set over a saucepan or wok of boiling water. Steam for 5 minutes, or until heated through. Serve with the reserved pine nut sauce.

Steamed snapper with burghul pilaff and pine nut sauce

6 x 150 g (5½ oz) snapper fillets, or other firm white fish fillets
1 teaspoon finely grated lemon rind
155 g (5½ oz/1 cup) pine nuts
1 small garlic clove, peeled
100 ml (3½ fl oz) lemon juice
100 ml (3½ fl oz) verjuice or white wine
1 tablespoon olive oil
chopped flat-leaf (Italian) parsley, to garnish
lemon wedges, to serve

Burghul pilaff

50 g (1¾ oz) butter
1 onion, finely diced
1 fennel bulb, about 250 g (9 oz), trimmed, cored and finely diced
1 teaspoon cumin seeds
½ teaspoon ground allspice
½ teaspoon chilli flakes
350 g (12 oz/2 cups) coarse burghul (bulgur)
750 ml (26 fl oz/3 cups) chicken stock
690 ml (24 fl oz) jar tomato passata (puréed tomatoes)
75 g (2½ oz/½ cup) currants
1 teaspoon honey
1½ teaspoons pomegranate molasses (optional)
45 g (1½ oz/½ cup) flaked almonds, toasted

To make the burghul pilaff, melt the butter in a large saucepan over medium–low heat. Add the onion and fennel and a pinch of salt and sauté for 5 minutes, or until translucent.

Add the spices and cook, stirring, for 30 seconds, then add the burghul, stock, passata, currants, honey and pomegranate molasses, if using. Reduce the heat to very low, then cover and cook for 20–25 minutes, or until the burghul has absorbed the liquid and is tender. Remove from the heat and leave to stand for 5 minutes. Just before serving, stir the almonds through.

Place the fish fillets in a steamer basket, in a single layer. Sprinkle with the lemon rind and some sea salt and freshly ground black pepper. Set over a saucepan or wok of boiling water and steam for 5 minutes, or until the fish is just cooked through.

Crush the pine nuts and garlic with a pinch of salt using a mortar and pestle or a small food processor. Mix in the lemon juice, verjuice and olive oil and stir or process until smooth, adding a teaspoon of cold water if necessary.

For the next day, reserve 2 fish fillets, half the burghul pilaff and half the pine nut sauce for the snapper pilaff rolls. (The fish can be refrigerated in an airtight container overnight; the other ingredients can be refrigerated in airtight containers for up to 2 days, but are not suitable for freezing.)

Spoon the remaining pilaff onto serving plates. Top with the remaining fish fillets. Drizzle with the remaining pine nut sauce, sprinkle with parsley and serve with lemon wedges.

Preparation time: 30 minutes · Cooking time: 35 minutes · Serves: 4

Preparation time: 15 minutes   **Cooking time:** 3 hours 20 minutes   **Serves:** 4

Slow-roasted lamb with honey pomegranate onion jam

2 tablespoons olive oil
1.75 kg (3 lb 14 oz) leg of lamb
2 onions, diced
2 garlic cloves, crushed
1 carrot, diced
2 celery stalks, sliced
2 thyme sprigs, plus extra, to garnish
1 dried red chilli
1 cinnamon stick
3 tomatoes, chopped
1 tablespoon finely grated lemon rind
250 ml (9 fl oz/1 cup) white wine
750 ml (26 fl oz/3 cups) chicken stock
800 g (1 lb 12 oz) butternut pumpkin
  (squash), peeled, seeded and cut
  into large chunks

Honey pomegranate onion jam

1 tablespoon olive oil
6 onions, thinly sliced
60 ml (2 fl oz/¼ cup) pomegranate
  molasses
125 ml (4 fl oz/½ cup) orange juice
2 tablespoons red wine vinegar
2 tablespoons honey

Preheat the oven to 150°C (300°F/Gas 2).

Heat the olive oil in a large flameproof baking dish over medium heat. Add the lamb leg and sear on each side for 3 minutes, or until browned. Remove to a plate.

Add the onion, garlic, carrot, celery and thyme to the dish and cook for 3 minutes, or until the onion starts to soften. Add the chilli, cinnamon stick, tomatoes, lemon rind, wine and stock. Bring to the boil and simmer for 1 minute.

Add the lamb to the dish and cover with foil. Transfer to the oven and bake for 2 hours.

After 2 hours, add the pumpkin to the dish, then cover and bake for a further 1 hour, or until the lamb and pumpkin are very tender.

Meanwhile, make the honey pomegranate onion jam. Heat the olive oil in a large saucepan over medium heat. Add the onion and cook for 10–15 minutes, or until the onion is soft, stirring often. Add the pomegranate molasses, orange juice, vinegar and honey and stir until well combined. Reduce the heat to low and simmer for 20 minutes, or until the mixture is sticky and thick.

Strain the lamb pan juices remaining in the baking dish through a fine sieve.

Carve the lamb and arrange on serving plates. Drizzle with the strained pan juices and garnish with extra thyme sprigs. Serve with the roasted pumpkin and some of the honey pomegranate onion jam.

For the next day, reserve the leftover lamb and honey pomegranate onion jam for the lamb wraps. (The ingredients can be refrigerated in airtight containers for up to 3 days, but are not suitable for freezing.)

Lamb wraps with feta
Serves 4

In a bowl, combine 1 finely chopped Lebanese (short) cucumber, 2 finely chopped tomatoes and 75 g (2½ oz/½ cup) crumbled feta cheese. Spread 4 mountain bread slices with 1 tablespoon of hummus each, then spoon the feta salad down the centre of each slice. Top with slices of the reserved lamb, and some reserved honey pomegranate onion jam. Fold in the sides, then roll the wraps up firmly. Slice in half on an angle and serve.

Chicken croquettes

Serves 4–6 (makes 12)

Scrub 500 g (1 lb 2 oz) sebago or other all-purpose potatoes and chop into chunks. Cook in a saucepan of boiling water until tender, then drain well. Return to the pan over low heat for 3–4 minutes to dry the potatoes, shaking the pan often. Mash the potatoes well and set aside. Cook 125 g (4½ oz) finely chopped rindless bacon slices in a small frying pan for 3 minutes, or until golden. Add to the potato mixture with the reserved chicken stuffing and reserved chicken mixture and stir to combine well. Season to taste with sea salt and freshly ground black pepper. Using wet hands, shape the potato mixture into 12 croquettes, using about 55 g (2 oz/¼ cup) for each. Dip each croquette in plain (all-purpose) flour, then into 2 beaten eggs, and finally in 60 g (2¼ oz/1 cup) panko (Japanese breadcrumbs). Arrange the croquettes on a baking tray and spray with olive oil cooking spray. Bake for 30 minutes, or until browned lightly. In a small bowl, combine 125 g (4½ oz/½ cup) sour cream, 1 tablespoon lemon juice and 2 tablespoons finely snipped chives. Serve with the hot croquettes, with a green salad.

Chicken and leek pie

2 large barbecued chickens, with stuffing
30 g (1 oz) butter
1 leek, white part only, rinsed well and thinly sliced
2 carrots, finely chopped
1 garlic clove, crushed
2 teaspoons thyme
2 tablespoons plain (all-purpose) flour
125 ml (4 fl oz/½ cup) white wine
500 ml (17 fl oz/2 cups) milk, plus extra, for brushing
1 sheet frozen puff pastry, thawed
1 small handful baby rocket (arugula)
1 small fennel bulb, about 250 g (9 oz), thinly sliced
2 tablespoons olive oil
1 tablespoon white wine vinegar

Preheat the oven to 180°C (350°F/Gas 4).

Remove the meat from the chickens and roughly shred into a large bowl. Take about 100 g (3½ oz/¾ cup) of the chicken stuffing and mix it through the shredded chicken.

For the next day, reserve the remaining stuffing and 700 g (1 lb 9 oz/3 cups) of the shredded chicken mixture for the croquettes. (The ingredients can be refrigerated in airtight containers for up to 2 days, but are not suitable for freezing.)

Melt the butter in a large frying pan over medium heat. Add the leek and carrot and sauté for 5 minutes, or until softened. Add the garlic and thyme and cook, stirring, for 1 minute.

Sprinkle the flour over and cook, stirring, for 2 minutes. Stir in the wine and bring to a simmer, stirring constantly to prevent lumps forming. Reduce the heat to low and simmer, stirring often, for 3 minutes. Add the milk and stir until the mixture simmers and thickens.

Add the sauce to the remaining chicken mixture and stir to combine. Spoon the mixture into a 23 cm (9 inch) round pie dish. Place the puff pastry sheet over the top, trim the edge, then crimp or pleat the edge for a neat finish. (Alternatively, use four individual ramekins or small baking dishes, and cut out four rounds from the puff pastry as lids.)

Brush the pastry with a little extra milk. Set the pie on a baking tray and bake for 20 minutes, or until the pastry is deep golden.

Just before serving, place the rocket and fennel in a bowl, drizzle with the combined oil and vinegar and toss gently to combine. Serve with the hot pie.

Preparation time: 30 minutes **Cooking time:** 40 minutes **Serves:** 4

Preparation time: 10 minutes   **Cooking time:** 25 minutes   **Serves:** 4

Smoked fish with horseradish cream sauce

1.25 kg (2 lb 12 oz) smoked fish
    fillets, such as cod
1 tablespoon vegetable oil
50 g (1¾ oz) butter
1 onion, finely diced
1 leek, white part only, rinsed well
    and finely diced
50 g (1¾ oz/⅓ cup) plain
    (all-purpose) flour
2 tablespoons bottled horseradish,
    or to taste
100 ml (3½ fl oz) cream
steamed spinach, to serve
boiled potatoes, to serve
2 tablespoons snipped chives

Poaching stock
600 ml (21 fl oz) milk
1 onion, sliced
1 carrot, sliced
1 bay leaf

Put the poaching stock ingredients in a large shallow saucepan or deep frying pan with 400 ml (14 fl oz) water and bring to the boil. Add the fish fillets, then reduce the heat to low and simmer for 10 minutes, or until the fish is tender.

Reserving the poaching stock, remove the fish to a warm bowl. Cover with a sheet of greased baking paper and keep warm.

Heat the oil and butter in a saucepan over medium heat. Add the onion and leek and sauté for 5 minutes, or until softened. Sprinkle the flour over and cook, stirring, for 1 minute, or until smooth.

Strain 500 ml (17 fl oz/2 cups) of the poaching stock into the saucepan. Stir over medium–low heat for 5 minutes, or until thickened. Stir in the horseradish and cream and season to taste with sea salt and freshly ground black pepper.

For the next day, reserve 4 fish fillets and 250 ml (9 fl oz/1 cup) of the horseradish cream sauce for the vol au vents. (The ingredients can be refrigerated in airtight containers for up to 2 days, but are not suitable for freezing.)

Serve the remaining fish with steamed spinach and boiled potatoes, drizzled with the remaining horseradish cream sauce and sprinkled with the chives.

Smoked fish vol au vents
Serves 4 (makes 12)

Preheat the oven to 180°C (350°F/Gas 4). Remove the skin from the reserved fish fillets, then flake the flesh with a fork and set aside. Gently heat the reserved horseradish cream sauce in a saucepan over medium heat; if the sauce is too thick, stir in about 1 tablespoon milk. Add the fish, 1 tablespoon snipped chives and 1 tablespoon chopped parsley and cook for 5 minutes, or until the mixture is warmed through. Spoon the mixture into twelve 6 cm (2½ inch) vol au vent cases. Place the vol au vents on a baking tray and bake for 15–20 minutes, or until heated through. Serve hot, with a salad.

Lamb samosas

Serves 4–6 (makes 20)

Preheat the oven to 190ºC (375ºF/ Gas 5). In a bowl, mix together the reserved lamb, reserved yoghurt-almond sauce, 2 tablespoons chopped mint and 80 g (2¾ oz/ ½ cup) thawed frozen peas. Season to taste with sea salt and a squeeze of lemon juice. Thaw 4 frozen butter puff pastry sheets, then cut out 20 pastry rounds, each about 8½ cm (3½ inches) across. Place a tablespoon of the lamb filling in the middle of each round, then lightly brush the edges with 1 lightly beaten egg yolk mixed with 1 tablespoon water. Fold the edges over to form a semi-circle, then use a fork to seal. Brush the tops with the egg yolk mixture and sprinkle with cumin seeds. Prick the tops of each samosa several times with a small sharp knife, then place on a greased baking tray. Bake for 25 minutes, or until puffed and golden. Meanwhile, in a bowl, combine 375 g (13 oz/1½ cups) plain yoghurt, 1 tablespoon finely chopped mint and 1 peeled and grated Lebanese (short) cucumber. Season to taste with sea salt and freshly ground black pepper and serve with the warm samosas.

Pot roast Indian lamb

2.25 kg (5 lb) leg of lamb, trimmed
  of fat and sinew
30 g (1 oz) ghee
1 onion, finely chopped
450 g (1 lb/2¼ cups) basmati rice
steamed silverbeet (Swiss chard),
  to serve
lemon wedges, to serve

Yoghurt-almond marinade
500 g (1 lb 2 oz/2 cups) plain yoghurt
1 onion, chopped
2 garlic cloves, finely chopped
10 cm (4 inch) piece of fresh ginger,
  peeled and grated
70 g (2½ oz/⅔ cup) ground almonds
2 teaspoons sea salt
½ teaspoon chilli flakes
1 tablespoon garam masala
1 teaspoon ground cumin

Using a small knife, make several long incisions in the lamb. Place the lamb in a deep bowl.

Put the yoghurt-almond marinade ingredients in a food processor and blend until a smooth paste forms. Spread the marinade evenly over the lamb, pushing it into the cuts. Cover and marinate in the refrigerator for 24 hours.

The next day, preheat the oven to 180°C (350°C/Gas 4) and bring the lamb to room temperature.

Set the lamb in a large casserole dish or deep roasting tin, then pour any remaining yoghurt-almond marinade over the lamb. Cover tightly with the casserole lid, or seal the roasting tin with foil. Bake for 1½ hours.

Remove the lid or foil, then baste the lamb with the yoghurt-almond sauce. Bake for a further 30–45 minutes, basting the lamb twice more during cooking. Remove from the oven, cover with foil and leave to rest in a warm place for 15 minutes before carving.

Meanwhile, heat the ghee in a saucepan over medium heat. Add the onion and sauté for 5 minutes, or until softened and starting to colour. Add the rice and cook, stirring, for 2–3 minutes, or until translucent. Add 875 ml (30 fl oz/3½ cups) water and bring to a simmer, then cover and cook over medium–low heat for 15 minutes, or until the rice is cooked and holes appear over the surface. Remove from the heat and leave to stand for 10 minutes.

Carve the lamb into thick slices and divide among serving plates. Spoon the yoghurt-almond sauce over and serve with the rice, steamed silverbeet and lemon wedges.

For the next day, reserve about 265 g (9¼ oz/ 1½ cups) of shredded lamb and 2½ tablespoons of the yoghurt-almond sauce for the lamb samosas. (The ingredients can be refrigerated in airtight containers for up to 3 days, but are not suitable for freezing.)

Preparation time: 30 minutes
plus 24 hours marinating

Cooking time: 2 hours 15 minutes

Serves: 4–6

Preparation time: 20 minutes ☀ Cooking time: 3 hours 35 minutes ☀ Serves: 4

Risoni, beef and walnut pilaff

80 ml (2½ fl oz/⅓ cup) olive oil

1.25 kg (2 lb 12 oz) beef chuck steak, trimmed of fat and sinew, then cut into 5 cm (2 inch) chunks

500 ml (17 fl oz/2 cups) beef stock

1 large onion, thinly sliced

500 g (1 lb 2 oz) pumpkin (winter squash), peeled, seeded and finely chopped

1 small eggplant (aubergine), finely chopped

3 teaspoons baharat spice mix (available from spice shops; or mix together 1 teaspoon paprika, 1 teaspoon ground cumin, 1 teaspoon ground coriander and a pinch each of ground cloves, cinnamon and cardamom)

1 teaspoon ground cumin

1 teaspoon ground fennel seeds

385 g (13½ oz/2 cups) risoni

220 g (7¾ oz/½ large bunch) English spinach, washed and trimmed, then shredded

60 g (2¼ oz/½ cup) chopped walnut pieces, lightly toasted

lemon wedges, to serve

Heat 1 tablespoon of the olive oil in a large heavy-based saucepan over high heat. Add the beef in batches and fry for 5 minutes, or until browned all over, turning often and removing each batch to a plate.

Return all the meat to the saucepan. Add the stock and 375 ml (13 fl oz/1½ cups) water and bring to a simmer. Cover and cook over low heat for 2½ hours, or until the beef is tender.

Remove the beef from the liquid in the pan. When cool enough to handle, shred the meat. Reserve 750 ml (26 fl oz/3 cups) of the cooking liquid. Discard the remaining stock, or freeze for use in another recipe.

Heat the remaining oil in a large frying pan. Add the onion and sauté for 3 minutes, then add the pumpkin and eggplant and cook over medium heat for 5–7 minutes, or until lightly browned, stirring often. Transfer the vegetables to a bowl.

Add the spices and risoni to the pan and cook, stirring, for 3 minutes, or until the risoni is coated in the spices. Return the vegetables to the pan with the shredded beef and the reserved cooking liquid. Bring to the boil, reduce the heat to low, then cover and simmer for 12 minutes, or until the risoni is tender. Season to taste with sea salt and freshly ground black pepper.

Stir in the spinach and cook for 2 minutes, or until the spinach has just wilted.

For the next day, reserve 700 g (1 lb 9 oz/ 2 cups) of the beef mixture for the pie filling. (The beef mixture can be refrigerated in an airtight container for up to 3 days, but is not suitable for freezing.)

Spoon the beef mixture into serving bowls. Sprinkle with the walnuts and serve with lemon wedges.

Eggplant, beef and risoni pie
Serves 4

Cut 2 large eggplant (aubergine) into slices about 5 mm (¼ inch) thick. Layer the slices in a large colander, sprinkling with sea salt as you go, then allow to stand for 30 minutes. Meanwhile, preheat the oven to 180°C (350°F/ Gas 4). Rinse the eggplant well, then pat dry with kitchen paper. Brush each slice with olive oil and cook in batches in a large frying pan for 1 minute on each side, or until lightly browned. Cool slightly. In a large bowl, combine the reserved beef mixture, 4 finely chopped vine-ripened tomatoes and 1 large handful finely chopped flat-leaf (Italian) parsley; set aside. Grease a 22 cm (8½ inch) springform cake tin, then cover the base and side with the eggplant slices. Spoon the beef mixture into the middle, then fold the eggplant slices over to enclose the filling. Top the pie with any remaining eggplant slices. Set on a baking tray and bake for 30 minutes, or until browned lightly. Remove from the oven and allow to cool in the tin for 15 minutes, then serve with lemon wedges and a green salad.

Red lentil and pea dhal

Serves 4 as a light meal

Heat 1 teaspoon vegetable oil in a saucepan over medium heat. Add 2 teaspoons Indian curry paste (such as korma) and cook, stirring, for 2 minutes, or until fragrant. Add the reserved lentil mixture, reserved peas and 250 ml (9 fl oz/1 cup) water and bring to the boil. Reduce the heat to low and cook for 20 minutes, or until the lentils are very soft and breaking up, stirring occasionally. Mash the peas and lentils with the back of a spoon, then stir in 1 tablespoon lemon juice and 4 tablespoons chopped coriander (cilantro) leaves. Spoon into warm serving bowls. Working quickly, heat a knob of butter in a small frying pan over medium heat until it begins to sizzle. Add 1 teaspoon cumin seeds, then immediately pour over the dhal. Serve with naan bread.

Lamb cutlets with spicy red lentils

2 tablespoons vegetable oil, plus extra, for brushing
1 onion, finely chopped
1 garlic clove, finely chopped
2 cm (¾ inch) piece of fresh ginger, peeled and finely chopped
1 teaspoon ground cumin
1 teaspoon curry powder
½ teaspoon ground turmeric
1 teaspoon sea salt
500 g (1 lb 2 oz/2 cups) red lentils
3 tomatoes, diced
100 ml (3½ fl oz) lemon juice
450 g (1 lb/3 cups) fresh shelled peas or frozen peas
8 French-trimmed lamb cutlets
40 g (1½ oz) butter
1 small handful mint leaves

Heat the oil in a saucepan over medium heat. Add the onion and sauté for 5 minutes, or until softened. Add the garlic and ginger and cook for 2 minutes, then stir in the spices, sea salt and lentils to combine. Add the tomatoes and cook for 2 minutes. Add the lemon juice and 625 ml (21½ fl oz/2½ cups) water and bring to the boil. Reduce the heat to medium–low and cook for 5–10 minutes, or until the lentils are just tender. Don't overcook the lentils or they will break up and become mushy. Remove from the heat.

Meanwhile, bring a saucepan of salted water to the boil. Add the peas and simmer for 3–5 minutes, or until just cooked. Drain and rinse under cold water, then drain again.

For the next day, reserve one-third of the lentil mixture and 150 g (5½ oz/1 cup) of the peas for the dhal. (The lentils can be refrigerated in an airtight container for up to 1 week, or frozen for up to 1 month; the peas can be refrigerated for up to 4 days.)

Meanwhile, heat a chargrill pan or barbecue hotplate to high. Brush the lamb cutlets with vegetable oil and season with sea salt and freshly ground black pepper. Cook the lamb for 2–3 minutes on each side for medium–rare, or until done to your liking. Cover loosely with foil and leave to rest in a warm place for 10 minutes.

Melt the butter in a saucepan over medium heat. Add the drained peas and mint and cook for 1 minute to heat through and wilt the mint. Season with freshly ground black pepper.

Spoon the lentils onto serving plates. Top each with two lamb cutlets and serve with the minted peas.

Preparation time: 15 minutes   **Cooking time:** 25 minutes   **Serves:** 4

Preparation time: 30 minutes   **Cooking time:** 3 hours 15 minutes   **Serves:** 4

Beef in red wine with prunes and dark chocolate

2 kg (4 lb 8 oz) beef chuck steak,
 cut into 5 cm (2 inch) chunks
80 ml (2½ fl oz/⅓ cup) extra virgin
 olive oil
3 onions, chopped
2 celery stalks, chopped
6 garlic cloves, thinly sliced
450 ml (16 fl oz) red wine
330 g (11½ oz/1½ cups) pitted prunes,
 chopped
2 cinnamon sticks
2 rosemary sprigs, plus extra chopped
 rosemary, to garnish
2 x 400 g (14 oz) tins chopped tomatoes
750 ml (26 fl oz/3 cups) beef stock
50 g (1¾ oz/⅓ cup) chopped good-
 quality dark chocolate (70% cocoa)
400 g (14 oz) cooked fresh pappardelle
 pasta
finely grated rind of 1 orange
grated parmesan, to serve
crusty bread, to serve

Preheat the oven to 170°C (325°F/Gas 3). Season the beef with sea salt and ground white pepper.

Heat 1 tablespoon of the olive oil in a large flameproof casserole dish over high heat. Add the beef in batches and cook for 4–5 minutes, or until browned all over, turning often and adding a little more oil as necessary. Remove each batch to a plate.

Heat the remaining oil in the dish over medium heat. Add the onion, celery and garlic and sauté for 10 minutes. Add the wine and boil for 5 minutes, or until reduced by half.

Return all the beef to the dish, along with the prunes, cinnamon sticks, rosemary sprigs, tomatoes and stock. Bring just to a simmer, then cover with a tight-fitting lid or a double layer of foil and transfer to the oven. Bake for 1½–2 hours, or until the beef is tender.

Remove the dish from the oven. If necessary, place some kitchen paper on the surface of the sauce to absorb any excess oil, repeating as necessary.

Using a slotted spoon, remove the beef from the sauce to a warm plate and cover with foil. Set aside while finishing the sauce.

Simmer the sauce remaining in the casserole dish over high heat for 20 minutes, or until reduced by half, stirring often. Return the beef to the casserole and allow to heat through. Add the chocolate, then stir until the chocolate has melted and the mixture is smooth.

For the next day, reserve half the beef for the cobbler. (The beef mixture can be refrigerated in an airtight container for up to 3 days, or frozen for up to 3 months.)

Spoon the remaining beef over bowls of cooked pappardelle pasta. Garnish with extra rosemary, grated orange rind and parmesan and serve with crusty bread.

Red wine beef and parmesan cobbler
Serves 4

Preheat the oven to 190°C (375°F/Gas 5). In a bowl, combine 225 g (8 oz/1½ cups) self-raising flour, 50 g (1¾ oz/ ½ cup) grated parmesan and 3 teaspoons chopped thyme or rosemary. Rub in 70 g (2½ oz) chopped butter until the mixture resembles breadcrumbs. Add 125 ml (4 fl oz/½ cup) buttermilk and work the mixture with your hands to form a firm dough. Turn the dough out onto a lightly floured surface and gently shape into a 23 cm (9 inch) square. Cut out rounds using a floured 6 cm (2½ inch) round cutter or a glass. Spoon the reserved beef mixture into a 20 cm (8 inch) square baking dish. Arrange the cobbler rounds over the top, overlapping them slightly. Bake for 30–40 minutes, or until browned on top. Serve hot.

Pork rice paper rolls with sesame ginger dipping sauce

Serves 4 (makes 16)

In a bowl, combine 2 teaspoons lightly toasted sesame seeds, 1 teaspoon soy sauce, 2 teaspoons grated fresh ginger, 2 tablespoons fish sauce, the juice of 3 limes and 2 tablespoons soft brown sugar. Stir until the sugar has dissolved; set aside. Soak 100 g (3½ oz) dried vermicelli noodles in cold water for 15 minutes, or until softened. Drain well, rinse under cold water and drain again; set aside. Keeping the ingredients separate, cut the reserved braised pork into strips; pick 1 handful each of coriander (cilantro) and mint leaves; trim 90 g (3¼ oz/1 cup) bean sprouts; cut 2 Lebanese (short) cucumbers into thin strips; and cut 4 spring onions (scallions) into thin matchsticks. Half-fill a bowl with warm water. Dip 1 rice paper round (measuring about 22 cm/8½ inches) into the water, then place on a clean surface. On the edge of each round place a small amount of the noodles, pork, coriander, mint, bean sprouts, cucumber and spring onion. Roll the rice paper up tightly, folding the edges in to enclose. Place on a clean damp tea towel (dish towel), covering with another damp tea towel. Repeat with more rice paper rolls and the remaining ingredients to make 16 rolls. Serve with the sesame ginger dipping sauce.

Ginger and star anise braised pork

1 tablespoon peanut oil
1.8 kg (4 lb) piece of pork neck
   (pork scotch fillet)
1 onion, chopped
2 carrots, chopped
6 cm (2½ inch) piece of fresh ginger,
   peeled and sliced into thin matchsticks
2 garlic cloves, thinly sliced
60 ml (2 fl oz/¼ cup) soy sauce
750 ml (26 fl oz/3 cups) chicken stock
125 ml (4 fl oz/½ cup) Chinese rice wine
2 tablespoons honey
3 star anise
steamed white rice, to serve
steamed snow peas (mangetout),
   to serve
2 spring onions (scallions), thinly sliced
   on the diagonal
1 small handful coriander (cilantro)
   leaves

Preheat the oven to 160°C (315°F/Gas 2–3).

Heat the peanut oil in a large flameproof casserole dish over medium heat. Add the pork neck and cook on each side for 4–5 minutes, or until browned. Remove to a plate.

Add the onion and carrot to the dish and sauté for 7 minutes, or until the onion has softened.

Stir in the ginger, garlic, soy sauce, stock, rice wine, honey and star anise. Return the pork to the dish and add enough water to come halfway up the side of the pork. Bring to the boil, remove from the heat and cover with a tight-fitting lid or a double layer of foil. Transfer to the oven and bake for 1 hour.

Turn the pork over, replace the lid or foil, then bake for a further 1 hour, or until the pork is tender. Transfer the pork to a plate, cover with foil and leave to rest in a warm place while finishing the sauce.

Strain the braising liquid into a clean saucepan. Bring to the boil over high heat, then reduce the heat to low and simmer for 8 minutes, or until reduced and thickened slightly.

Carve the pork into thick slices. Serve with steamed rice and snow peas, drizzled with the spiced sauce and sprinkled with the spring onion and coriander.

For the next day, reserve 300 g (10½ oz) of the braised pork for the rice paper rolls. (The pork can be refrigerated in an airtight container for up to 3 days, or frozen for up to 3 months.)

Preparation time: 15 minutes ❋ Cooking time: 2 hours 45 minutes ❋ Serves: 4

Roast chicken with lemon, honey, rosemary and zucchini

2 x 1.4 kg (3 lb 2 oz) chickens
2 lemons
60 g (2¼ oz) butter
3 garlic cloves, chopped
90 g (3¼ oz/¼ cup) honey
1 tablespoon chopped rosemary, plus
  2 rosemary sprigs
2 onions, cut into thick wedges
600 g (1 lb 5 oz) desiree or roasting
  potatoes, peeled and cut into 2 cm
  (¾ inch) chunks
2 tablespoons olive oil
4 zucchini (courgettes), about 500 g
  (1 lb 2 oz) in total, sliced 1 cm
  (½ inch) thick
2 teaspoons plain (all-purpose) flour
60 ml (2 fl oz/¼ cup) lemon juice
250 ml (9 fl oz/1 cup) chicken stock

Rinse the chickens inside and out and pat dry with kitchen paper. Sprinkle generously with sea salt and refrigerate for 1 hour.

Preheat the oven to 180°C (350°F/Gas 4). Finely grate the rind of the lemons, reserving the lemons. Place the grated rind in a small bowl, add the butter, garlic, honey and chopped rosemary and mix to a paste. Using your fingers, loosen the skin from the breast on each side of the chickens, to form two pockets on each chicken. Spread the butter mixture under the skin of each breast, then place the skin back over the breasts. Place 1 lemon and 1 rosemary sprig in each chicken cavity. Tie the legs together with kitchen string. Place the chickens in the centre of a large, flameproof roasting tin; arrange the onion and potato around them. Season the vegetables with sea salt and freshly ground black pepper and drizzle with the olive oil. Roast, uncovered, for 30 minutes.

Add the zucchini to the roasting tin and roast for another 20 minutes, or until the chickens are golden brown and the juices run clear when pierced with a skewer through a thigh and leg joint. (If the skin is browning too quickly, cover the birds loosely with foil.) Remove the chicken and vegetables to a platter, reserving the pan juices. Cover with foil and keep warm.

Place the roasting tin over medium heat. Sprinkle the flour over and stir well with a wooden spoon, scraping up any cooked-on bits. Add the lemon juice, stock and any juices from the resting chicken and cook for 1 minute. Bring to the boil and simmer, uncovered, for 2–3 minutes, or until the gravy has reduced by half and has thickened slightly.

For the next day, remove and reserve the meat from half of 1 chicken for the soup. (The chicken can be refrigerated in an airtight container for up to 2 days, but is not suitable for freezing.)

Carve the remaining chicken, reserving the bones and carcass for the soup. Serve with the roasted vegetables, drizzled with the gravy.

Chicken and zucchini soup
Serves 4

Place the reserved chicken bones and carcasses in a stockpot. Add 1 litre (35 fl oz/4 cups) water and 2 bay leaves. Bring to the boil over medium heat, then reduce the heat to low and simmer for 1 hour, skimming off any froth that rises to the surface. Strain the stock through a fine sieve into a bowl; you should have about 700 ml (24 fl oz). Set aside to cool slightly. Melt 20 g (¾ oz) butter in a large saucepan over medium heat. Add 1 finely chopped onion, 1 large finely chopped celery stalk and 2 crushed garlic cloves. Sauté for 5 minutes, or until softened. Sprinkle with 2 tablespoons plain (all-purpose) flour and cook, stirring, for 1 minute, or until smooth. Dice the reserved chicken meat and add to the saucepan with the reserved chicken stock and 500 g (1 lb 2 oz/3¼ cups) grated zucchini. Bring to the boil and cook for 5 minutes, or until the soup has thickened slightly. Stir in 250 ml (9 fl oz/1 cup) cream, reduce the heat to low and simmer for 2 minutes. Season to taste with sea salt and freshly ground black pepper. Serve garnished with snipped chives.

Roast vegetable and lentil soup

Serves 4–6

Melt 20 g (¾ oz) butter in a large saucepan over medium heat. Add 1 large chopped onion and 6 chopped bacon slices and sauté for 5 minutes, or until the onion has softened. Add 1 crushed garlic clove and cook, stirring, for 1 minute. Roughly chop the reserved roasted vegetables and add to the pan with 2 rosemary sprigs, 750 ml (26 fl oz/3 cups) chicken stock, a 400 g (14 oz) tin of chopped tomatoes and a rinsed and drained 400 g (14 oz) tin of lentils. Bring to the boil, then reduce the heat to medium and simmer, uncovered, for 10 minutes. Serve with a dollop of sour cream.

Warm vegetable and lentil salad

1.25 kg (2 lb 12 oz) kipfler (fingerling) potatoes, scrubbed and halved
1.25 kg (2 lb 12 oz) sweet potatoes, peeled and cut into 3 cm (1¼ inch) chunks
12 French shallots, peeled
350 g (12 oz/1 bunch) baby carrots, trimmed and scrubbed
1 large cauliflower, about 900 g (2 lb), cut into florets
80 ml (2½ fl oz/⅓ cup) olive oil
4 rindless bacon slices, about 160 g (5¾ oz) in total, chopped
400 g (14 oz) tin lentils, rinsed and drained
100 g (3½ oz) baby English spinach leaves

Dressing
125 ml (4 fl oz/½ cup) chicken stock
125 ml (4 fl oz/½ cup) cream
1½ tablespoons white wine
25 g (1 oz) crumbled blue cheese
25 g (1 oz/¼ cup) grated parmesan
125 g (4½ oz) chilled butter, chopped

Preheat the oven to 200°C (400°F/Gas 6). Grease and line two large baking trays with baking paper.

Arrange the potato and sweet potato in a single layer on one of the baking trays, and spread the shallots, carrots and cauliflower on the other. Drizzle each with 1½ tablespoons of the olive oil and turn to coat. Season with sea salt and freshly ground black pepper and roast for 50–60 minutes, or until golden and tender; remove the vegetables as they are cooked, as some may require less cooking time than others. Set aside to cool for 10 minutes.

For the next day, reserve half the roasted potato and sweet potato for the roast vegetable and lentil soup. (The vegetables can be refrigerated in an airtight container for up to 2 days, but are not suitable for freezing.)

Meanwhile, heat the remaining oil in a non-stick frying pan over medium heat. Add the bacon and sauté for 6–7 minutes, or until golden. Drain the bacon on kitchen paper, then transfer to a large bowl. Add the lentils, spinach and remaining roasted vegetables and toss gently to combine. Keep warm.

To make the dressing, pour the stock, cream and wine into a small saucepan and bring to the boil. Reduce the heat to medium–low and simmer for 5–10 minutes, or until reduced by half. Reduce the heat to low, then add the blue cheese and parmesan and stir to combine. Whisking constantly, add the butter a few pieces at a time, making sure it has emulsified into the sauce before adding more. Season to taste. Remove from the heat and cool to room temperature.

Drizzle some of the dressing over the warm roast vegetable salad and gently toss to combine. Divide the salad among serving plates and serve drizzled with the remaining dressing.

Preparation time: 20 minutes   **Cooking time:** 1 hour 15 minutes   **Serves:** 4–6

Preparation time: 10 minutes
plus 15 minutes soaking

Cooking time: 50 minutes

Serves: 6–8

Roasted ham with sweet potato and mustard fruits

3 kg (6 lb 12 oz) piece of semi-boneless
   shoulder ham
2 garlic cloves, crushed
2 teaspoons grated fresh ginger
115 g (4 oz/½ cup) soft brown sugar
2 tablespoons red wine vinegar
½ teaspoon ground cinnamon
125 ml (4 fl oz/½ cup) orange juice
4 carrots, cut into 4 cm (1½ inch)
   chunks
2 sweet potatoes, about 480 g (1 lb 1 oz)
   each, peeled and cut into 4 cm
   (1½ inch) chunks
1 tablespoon olive oil
rocket (arugula), to serve

Mustard fruits
450 g (1 lb) mixed dried fruits, such as
   apricots, figs and prunes
250 ml (9 fl oz/1 cup) white wine vinegar
115 g (4 oz/½ cup) caster (superfine)
   sugar
2 tablespoons brown mustard seeds
2 teaspoons hot English mustard
1 teaspoon sea salt
a large pinch of ground cloves

Preheat the oven to 180°C (350°F/Gas 4).

Place a sheet of baking paper in a large baking dish. Remove the rind from the ham. Using a small sharp knife, score the fat layer of the ham about 5 mm (¼ inch) deep, in a diamond pattern. Place the ham on a rack in the baking dish.

In a small saucepan, bring the garlic, ginger, sugar, vinegar, cinnamon and orange juice to the boil over medium heat. Reduce the heat to low and simmer for 5 minutes, or until thickened slightly. Set aside to cool.

Brush half the orange juice mixture over the ham. In a bowl, toss the carrot and sweet potato with the olive oil, then place in the bottom of the baking dish, underneath the ham.

Roast the ham and vegetables for 20 minutes. Brush the remaining glaze over the ham and roast for a further 25 minutes, or until the vegetables are tender and the ham is golden.

While the ham is roasting, prepare the mustard fruits. Cut any large fruits in half, then place all the fruit in a bowl and cover with hot water. Soak for 15 minutes, then strain the water, reserving 250 ml (9 fl oz/1 cup). Place the reserved liquid and all the remaining ingredients, except the fruit, in a small saucepan over medium heat. Simmer until the sugar has dissolved and the mixture is smooth. Increase the heat to high and boil for 5 minutes, stirring occasionally. Add the fruit, reduce the heat to low and simmer for 20 minutes, or until the fruit is soft. Spoon into a sterilised jar or container and cool.

Carve the ham into slices and serve with the roasted vegetables, mustard fruits and rocket.

For the next day, reserve 200 g (7 oz) of the ham and any remaining mustard fruits for the hash cakes. (The ham can be refrigerated in an airtight container for up to 2 days, but is not suitable for freezing. The mustard fruits can be refrigerated for up to 4 weeks.)

Glazed ham hash cakes
Serves 4

Place 600 g (1 lb 5 oz) peeled and quartered desiree potatoes in a large saucepan of cold salted water. Bring to the boil over high heat and cook for 15 minutes, or until tender. Drain and roughly mash the potatoes so they are still quite chunky; set aside to cool completely. Chop the reserved glazed ham and add to the potato with 1 small handful chopped parsley, 4 thinly sliced spring onions (scallions) and 1 lightly beaten egg. Stir to combine, then shape into 8 patties. Place on a tray lined with baking paper and refrigerate for 1 hour, or until firm. Dust each patty with plain (all-purpose) flour. Heat 2 tablespoons vegetable oil in a large non-stick frying pan over medium heat. Cook the patties for 3 minutes on each side, or until golden and crisp. Serve with the remaining mustard fruits and a green salad.

Lamb steaks with white bean and potato ragoût

Potato, white bean and pancetta soup

Serves 4

Warm the reserved ragoût in a saucepan over medium heat with 750 ml (26 fl oz/3 cups) chicken stock until just simmering. Purée the soup with a stick blender. Serve with chopped fresh herbs, warm crusty bread and freshly grated parmesan to taste. (This soup can also be frozen in an airtight container for up to 3 months.)

2 garlic cloves, peeled
1 rosemary sprig, plus extra leaves, to garnish
1 teaspoon finely grated lemon rind
2½ tablespoons lemon juice
80 ml (2½ fl oz/⅓ cup) olive oil
8 x 100 g (3½ oz) lamb leg steaks
100 g (3½ oz) pancetta or speck, in one piece, finely diced
2 onions, diced
1.25 kg (2 lb 12 oz) Dutch cream or nicola potatoes, peeled and cut into 1.5 cm (⅝ inch) chunks
500 ml (17 fl oz/2 cups) chicken stock
2 x 400 g (14 oz) tins cannellini beans, rinsed and drained
3 tablespoons chopped flat-leaf (Italian) parsley

In a small bowl, crush the garlic cloves with 1 teaspoon sea salt. Add the rosemary sprig, lemon rind, lemon juice and 1 tablespoon of the olive oil. Mix well, then pour into a large non-metallic dish. Add the lamb and turn to coat all over. Cover and marinate for 30 minutes.

Heat the remaining oil in a large frying pan over medium–low heat. Add the pancetta and onion and cook for 10–15 minutes, or until the onion is very soft, stirring occasionally.

Add the potato and cook for a further 3 minutes to absorb the flavours. Pour in the stock and cook for 12–15 minutes, or until the potato is tender. Stir in the cannellini beans and cook for 3 minutes to heat through. Discard the rosemary sprig, then stir in the parsley.

Meanwhile, preheat a barbecue hotplate or chargrill pan to medium–high. Add the lamb steaks, reduce the heat to medium and cook for 2–3 minutes on each side for medium–rare, or until done to your liking.

For the next day, reserve half the bean and potato ragoût for the soup. (The ragoût can be refrigerated in an airtight container for up to 3 days, but is not suitable for freezing.)

Spoon the remaining bean and potato ragoût onto serving plates or into bowls. Top with the lamb, garnish with extra rosemary and serve.

Preparation time: 20 minutes
plus 30 minutes marinating

Cooking time: 40 minutes

Serves: 4

Preparation time: 20 minutes   **Cooking time:** 1 hour   **Serves:** 4

Classic meatballs

2 pieces (100 g/3½ oz) day-old Italian
  bread, crusts removed
125 ml (4 fl oz/½ cup) milk
600 g (1 lb 5 oz) minced (ground) beef
600 g (1 lb 5 oz) minced (ground) pork
100 g (3½ oz/1 cup) grated parmesan,
  plus extra, to serve
1½ tablespoons chopped rosemary
80 ml (2½ fl oz/⅓ cup) olive oil
4 garlic cloves, thinly sliced
2 x 400 g (14 oz) tins chopped tomatoes
400 g (14 oz) tin tomato passata
  (puréed tomatoes)
2 teaspoons caster (superfine) sugar
2 large handfuls baby English spinach
800 g (1 lb 12 oz) short pasta, such as
  calabresi, trofie or pasta twists

Soak the bread in the milk for 1 minute, or until softened. Gently squeeze out and discard the excess liquid. Place the bread in a bowl with the beef, pork, parmesan and rosemary. Season with sea salt and freshly ground black pepper. Mix using your hands until well combined.

For the next day, reserve half the meat mixture for the meatball, basil and parmesan bake.

Heat the olive oil in a large frying pan over low heat. Add the garlic and sauté for 4–5 minutes, or until the garlic is just becoming golden. Remove half the oil and garlic mixture and reserve for the meatball sauce.

Strain the remaining oil, reserving the oil. Add the garlic to the remaining mince mixture. Roll heaped tablespoons of the mixture into balls.

Heat the strained garlic oil in the frying pan over medium–high heat and fry the meatballs in batches for 4–5 minutes, turning regularly, until browned all over. Remove each batch to a plate.

Add the remaining oil mixture to the frying pan with the tomatoes, passata and sugar. Season to taste and cook over medium heat for 30–35 minutes, or until the sauce has reduced by almost half. Add the meatballs and cook for a further 10 minutes, or until the meatballs are cooked through. Stir in the spinach and cook for another 1 minute, or until wilted.

Meanwhile, add the pasta to a large pot of rapidly boiling salted water and cook according to the packet instructions until al dente. Drain well.

For the next day, reserve half the pasta for the meatball, basil and parmesan bake.

Divide the remaining pasta among four serving bowls, top with the meatballs and serve.

Meatball, basil and parmesan bake
Serves 4

Preheat the oven to 170°C (325°F/Gas 3). Melt 60 g (2¼ oz) butter in a saucepan over medium heat. Add 50 g (1¾ oz/⅓ cup) plain (all-purpose) flour and cook, stirring, for 2 minutes. Add 600 ml (21 fl oz) milk and whisk to combine well. Whisking constantly to prevent lumps forming, bring the mixture to a simmer, then cook for 5 minutes, or until thickened, whisking occasionally. Meanwhile, mix the reserved meatballs and pasta with 1 large handful torn basil and place in a 2 litre (70 fl oz/8 cup) shallow baking dish. Pour the white sauce over, scatter with grated parmesan and bake for 30 minutes, or until the topping is bubbling and starting to colour. Serve hot.

Indian curried lamb

Curried lamb and egg bake
Serves 4

Preheat the oven to 180°C
(350°F/Gas 4). Spoon the reserved
lamb curry into four 250 ml
(9 fl oz/1 cup) ramekins. In a bowl,
mix together the reserved rice,
80 g (2¾ oz/⅓ cup) Greek yoghurt
and 1 beaten egg, then divide
among the ramekins. Bake for
15–20 minutes, or until browned
on top. Serve with a green salad.

1.25 kg (2 lb 12 oz) boneless lamb leg,
  cut into 2.5 cm (1 inch) chunks
80 g (2¾ oz/⅓ cup) Indian curry
  paste, such as rogan josh
2 tablespoons vegetable oil
1 onion, chopped
2 garlic cloves, crushed
1 red chilli, seeded and diced
2 x 400 g (14 oz) tins chopped tomatoes
400 g (14 oz/2 cups) basmati rice
300 g (10½ oz) green beans, trimmed
coriander (cilantro) leaves, to serve
chopped toasted flaked almonds,
  to serve

In a large bowl, combine the lamb and curry
paste. Mix until the lamb is well coated, then
cover and marinate in the refrigerator for 2 hours.

Heat the oil in a large saucepan over medium
heat. Add the onion and sauté for 3–4 minutes,
or until the onion is starting to brown. Add
the garlic and chilli and cook, stirring, for
2–3 minutes, or until fragrant.

Add the lamb and cook for 5–6 minutes, or
until browned all over, turning regularly. Add
the tomatoes and 250 ml (9 fl oz/1 cup) water
and simmer for 1 hour, or until the lamb is very
tender. Season to taste with sea salt and freshly
ground black pepper.

Meanwhile, rinse the rice under cold
running water until the water runs clear. Place
the rice and 375 ml (13 fl oz/1½ cups) cold
water in a large saucepan, then cover and cook
over low heat for 20–25 minutes, or until the
rice is tender.

Bring another saucepan of water to the boil.
Add the beans and cook for 2–3 minutes, or
until bright green and tender. Rinse under cold
running water.

For the next day, reserve half the beans, half
the lamb curry and 280 g (10 oz/1½ cups) of
the rice for the curried lamb and egg bake. Chop
the reserved beans and mix them through the
reserved lamb curry. (The ingredients can be
refrigerated in airtight containers for 1–2 days,
but are not suitable for freezing.)

Slice the remaining beans on the diagonal.
Divide the remaining rice among serving bowls,
scatter the beans over and top with the remaining
curry. Sprinkle with coriander and chopped
toasted almonds and serve.

Preparation time: 20 minutes
plus 2 hours marinating

Cooking time: 1 hour 15 minutes

Serves: 4

Chorizo and capsicum paella

80 ml (2½ fl oz/⅓ cup) olive oil
2 chorizo sausages, sliced 1 cm
  (½ inch) thick
2 large onions, thinly sliced
2 large red capsicums (peppers),
  thinly sliced
4 large vine-ripened tomatoes,
  seeded and chopped
4 garlic cloves, finely chopped
2 teaspoons Spanish smoked paprika
330 g (11½ oz/1½ cups) arborio rice
750 ml (26 fl oz/3 cups) chicken or
  vegetable stock, heated
125 g (4½ oz) baby green beans,
  cut into 3 cm (1¼ inch) lengths
3 tablespoons chopped flat-leaf (Italian)
  parsley
lemon wedges, to serve

Heat half the olive oil in a large, deep heavy-based frying pan or paella pan over low heat. Add the sausages and cook for 5 minutes, or until golden, stirring regularly. Remove to a bowl.

Heat the remaining oil in the pan. Add the onion and sauté for 15 minutes, or until golden. Add the capsicum and sauté for 10 minutes. Stir in the tomatoes, garlic and paprika and cook, stirring occasionally, for 15 minutes. Stir in the rice until well combined.

Return the sausages to the pan with half the stock. Stir the mixture well, then simmer over medium–low heat for 10 minutes. Stir in the remaining stock, scatter the beans over the top and reduce the heat to low. Cook without stirring for 30 minutes, or until the liquid is absorbed and the rice is tender.

Remove the paella from the heat and allow to stand for 5 minutes.

For the next day, reserve half the paella for the spinach rice pie. (The paella can be refrigerated in an airtight container for 1–2 days, but is not suitable for freezing.)

Scatter the remaining paella with the parsley and serve with lemon wedges.

Spinach rice pie
Serves 4

Preheat the oven to 180°C (350°F/ Gas 4). Mix 1 lightly beaten egg through the reserved paella mixture. Press two-thirds of the mixture over the base and side of an oiled ceramic 22 cm (8½ inch) pie dish. Fill with 2 handfuls baby English spinach leaves, then scatter with 30 g (1 oz/⅓ cup) grated pecorino cheese and 80 g (2¾ oz/⅔ cup) crumbled goat's cheese. Spread the remaining paella mixture over the top to cover, then press to seal the edges. Bake for 35 minutes, or until the crust is set and golden. Serve warm, cut into wedges.

Chicken, pancetta and pea risotto
Serves 4

Remove the meat from the reserved chicken thighs; thinly slice and set aside. In a saucepan, bring 1.25 litres (44 fl oz/5 cups) chicken stock to the boil; remove from the heat and keep hot. Heat 1 tablespoon olive oil in a saucepan over medium–low heat. Add 1 diced onion and 100 g (3½ oz) thinly sliced pancetta and sauté for 5 minutes. Stir in 2 crushed garlic cloves, then add 300 g (10½ oz/1⅓ cups) arborio rice and stir well to coat the rice. Add 125 ml (4 fl oz/½ cup) white wine and cook, stirring, for 2 minutes. Add a ladleful of the hot stock and stir constantly for 5 minutes, or until most of the liquid has evaporated. Add the remaining stock, a ladleful at a time, stirring until all the liquid has been absorbed before adding more stock. With the last addition of stock, add the sliced chicken and 155 g (5½ oz/1 cup) thawed frozen peas. Remove from the heat, stir in 50 g (1¾ oz/½ cup) grated parmesan and allow to stand for 2 minutes before serving.

Stuffed chicken thighs with pancetta

100 g (3½ oz) pancetta, thinly sliced
2 anchovy fillets
4 garlic cloves, finely chopped
1 tablespoon finely chopped sage, plus extra leaves, to garnish
20 g (¾ oz) unsalted butter
50 g (1¾ oz/½ cup) grated parmesan
8 chicken thighs, bone and skin on, trimmed of excess fat
6 desiree potatoes, peeled and cut into large chunks
1 tablespoon olive oil
125 ml (4 fl oz/½ cup) white wine

Preheat the oven to 200°C (400°F/Gas 6).

Combine the pancetta, anchovies, garlic, sage, butter and parmesan in a food processor and blend until a paste forms.

Gently place your finger under the skin of each chicken thigh to make a small pocket for the pancetta stuffing. Place 1 tablespoon of the stuffing into each pocket, then press firmly to attach the skin to the stuffing.

Place the potatoes in a baking dish and drizzle with the olive oil. Season with sea salt and freshly ground black pepper and bake for 10 minutes.

Place the chicken thighs in another large baking dish in one layer, skin side up. Season well, then transfer to the oven and bake with the potatoes for 20 minutes.

Pour the wine into the chicken dish and bake for a further 15 minutes, or until the chicken is cooked through and the potatoes are golden.

For the next day, reserve 4 chicken thighs for the chicken, pancetta and pea risotto. (The chicken can be refrigerated in an airtight container for up to 3 days, but is not suitable for freezing.)

Arrange the potatoes and remaining chicken thighs on serving plates. Skim the excess fat from the chicken pan juices. Drizzle the juices over the chicken, garnish with extra sage and serve.

✳ **Preparation time:** 20 minutes   ✳ **Cooking time:** 45 minutes   ✳ **Serves:** 4

Preparation time: 15 minutes   **Cooking time:** 2 hours   **Serves:** 4

Veal and vegetable stew with buttered noodles

60 ml (2 fl oz/¼ cup) olive oil
1.5 kg (3 lb 5 oz) veal shoulder, cut
   into 3 cm (1¼ inch) chunks
3 carrots, diced
3 celery stalks, sliced
2 onions, diced
2 garlic cloves, crushed
1½ tablespoons plain (all-purpose) flour
250 ml (9 fl oz/1 cup) white wine
400 g (14 oz) tin chopped tomatoes
125 ml (4 fl oz/½ cup) chicken stock
1 teaspoon dried oregano
finely grated rind and juice of 1 lemon
600 g (1 lb 5 oz) fresh tagliatelle
40 g (1½ oz) butter, melted
1 large handful flat-leaf (Italian) parsley,
   roughly chopped

Heat 1 tablespoon of the olive oil in a large heavy-based saucepan or flameproof casserole dish over medium heat. Add one-third of the veal and cook for 5 minutes, or until lightly browned, turning often. Transfer to a plate. Heat another 1 tablespoon of the oil and brown a second batch of veal; transfer to a plate, then repeat with the remaining oil and veal.

Add the carrot, celery, onion and garlic to the pan and sauté for 10 minutes, or until the onion is soft. Return all the veal to the pan, add the flour and stir continuously for 1 minute, until thoroughly combined.

Pour in the wine and cook, stirring, for 1 minute, or until the sauce is smooth and thick. Add the tomatoes, stock, oregano, lemon rind and lemon juice and bring to the boil. Reduce the heat to low, then cover and simmer for 1½ hours, or until the veal is very tender.

When the veal is nearly ready, add the tagliatelle to a large pot of rapidly boiling salted water and cook according to the packet instructions until al dente. Drain well.

For the next day, reserve about one-third of the veal casserole and about one-quarter of the tagliatelle for the veal and vegetable noodle cakes. (The ingredients can be refrigerated in airtight containers for up to 2 days, but are not suitable for freezing.)

Toss the melted butter through the remaining tagliatelle. Divide the tagliatelle and remaining veal among serving plates. Sprinkle with the parsley and serve.

Veal and vegetable noodle cakes with tomato and spinach salad
Serves 4

Place the reserved pasta and veal casserole in a large bowl. Add 40 g (1½ oz) softened butter, 3 lightly beaten eggs, 35 g (1¼ oz/¼ cup) drained capers, 55 g (2 oz/⅔ cup) fresh breadcrumbs, 50 g (1¾ oz/ ½ cup) grated parmesan and 1 handful chopped flat-leaf (Italian) parsley. Mix well, then form into 4 cakes and lightly coat with 40 g (1½ oz/½ cup) fresh breadcrumbs. Refrigerate for 4 hours to firm, or overnight. Preheat the oven to 200°C (400°F/ Gas 6). Spread 250 g (9 oz) halved cherry tomatoes on a lined baking tray. Drizzle with olive oil, season with sea salt and freshly ground black pepper and bake for 10 minutes, or until soft. Leave to cool, then toss in a bowl with 2 large handfuls baby English spinach leaves and 2 tablespoons balsamic vinegar; set aside. Meanwhile, bring the noodle cakes to room temperature. Heat 2 tablespoons olive oil in a large non-stick frying pan over medium heat. Cook the noodle cakes for 2–3 minutes on each side, or until golden. Serve with the tomato and spinach salad.

Fish pie
Serves 4

Preheat the oven to 180°C (350°F/ Gas 4). Heat 1 tablespoon olive oil in a large saucepan over medium–high heat. Add 1 thinly sliced red onion and 1 thinly sliced fennel bulb and sauté for 5 minutes, or until softened. Add 2 crushed garlic cloves and cook for 1 minute. Add 35 g (1¼ oz/¼ cup) plain (all-purpose) flour and cook, stirring, for 1 minute. Whisking constantly, add 250 ml (9 fl oz/ 1 cup) milk and 60 ml (2 fl oz/ ¼ cup) cream. Bring to the boil, reduce the heat to low and simmer, stirring occasionally, for 2 minutes, or until the mixture begins to thicken. Remove from the heat and stir in 2 teaspoons wholegrain mustard, 1 tablespoon lemon juice, 300 g (10½ oz) chopped smoked cod fillets and the reserved seafood mixture. Transfer to a 2 litre (70 fl oz/8 cup) baking dish. Thinly slice 500 g (1 lb 2 oz) potatoes and arrange the slices over the seafood mixture, overlapping them slightly. Brush the potato slices with 30 g (1 oz) melted butter and bake for 45 minutes, or until the potatoes are golden and the sauce is bubbling. Remove from the oven and allow the pie to stand for 10 minutes. Serve with a green salad.

Rustic fish stew

1 kg (2 lb 4 oz) small clams (vongole)
30 g (1 oz) butter
1 large onion, finely chopped
2 celery stalks, chopped
2 carrots, finely chopped
2 thyme sprigs
125 ml (4 fl oz/½ cup) white wine
375 ml (13 fl oz/1½ cups) chicken stock
1 kg (2 lb 4 oz) ling fillets, or other firm white fish fillets, thickly sliced
800 g (1 lb 12 oz) raw king prawns (shrimp), peeled and deveined, tails left intact
2 vine-ripened tomatoes, finely chopped
1 small handful dill, finely chopped
aïoli, to serve
crusty bread, to serve
lemon wedges, to serve

Place the clams in a bowl and cover with plenty of cold water. Cover and refrigerate for 2–3 hours. Drain the clams, discarding any that are open.

Melt the butter in a large heavy-based saucepan over medium–high heat. Add the onion, celery, carrot and thyme sprigs and sauté for 5 minutes, or until the vegetables have softened.

Pour in the wine and bring to the boil. Reduce the heat to low, then simmer for 5 minutes, or until half the wine has evaporated.

Pour in the stock and 250 ml (9 fl oz/1 cup) water. Bring back to the boil, then reduce the heat to low. Add the fish, prawns and clams. Cover and simmer for 3–4 minutes, shaking the pan occasionally.

Remove the pan from the heat. Leave the lid on and allow to stand for 3 minutes, or until the clams have opened and all the seafood is cooked through. Remove and discard any clams that haven't opened.

For the next day, drain off and reserve about 500 g (1 lb 2 oz/2 cups) of the seafood mixture (excluding the clams) for the fish pie. (The seafood mixture can be refrigerated in an airtight container for up to 2 days, but is not suitable for freezing.)

Stir the tomato and dill into the remaining stew, then divide among serving bowls. Top each bowl with aïoli, then serve with crusty bread and lemon wedges.

Preparation time: 30 minutes
plus 2–3 hours soaking

Cooking time: 15 minutes

Serves: 4

Preparation time: 30 minutes   Cooking time: 40 minutes   Serves: 4

Lamb, raisin and orange pilaff

1 kg (2 lb 4 oz) merguez sausages,
  or other spicy lamb sausages
2 tablespoons olive oil
1 large onion, thinly sliced
2 garlic cloves, crushed
2 teaspoons ground allspice
1 tablespoon chopped oregano
1 long, wide orange zest strip
1 dried bay leaf
60 g (2¼ oz/½ cup) raisins
400 g (14 oz/2 cups) basmati rice
500 ml (17 fl oz/2 cups) chicken stock
2 large tomatoes, finely chopped
125 g (4½ oz/½ cup) Greek yoghurt

Pistachio gremolata
90 g (3¼ oz/⅔ cup) chopped
  pistachio nuts
1 large handful flat-leaf (Italian) parsley,
  finely chopped
1 teaspoon finely grated orange rind

Remove and discard the skins from the sausages. Heat 1 tablespoon of the olive oil in a large flameproof casserole dish over medium–high heat. Add the sausage meat and cook for 10 minutes, or until lightly browned, stirring to break up any large lumps. Remove to a plate.

Drain off any excess fat from the dish. Add the remaining oil and heat over medium heat. Add the onion and sauté for 5 minutes, or until softened, then add the garlic, allspice, oregano, orange zest strip, bay leaf and raisins. Cook, stirring, for 1 minute, or until fragrant. Add the rice and stir to coat.

Return the sausage meat to the dish with the stock, tomatoes and 500 ml (17 fl oz/2 cups) water. Bring to the boil, then reduce the heat to low. Cover and simmer for 15 minutes, or until the rice is tender.

Meanwhile, combine the pistachio gremolata ingredients in a small bowl.

For the next day, reserve 600 g (1 lb 5 oz/ 3 cups) of the pilaff for the stuffed capsicums. (The pilaff can be refrigerated in an airtight container for up to 3 days, but is not suitable for freezing.)

Serve the pilaff with a dollop of yoghurt, sprinkled with the pistachio gremolata.

Capsicums stuffed with pilaff
Serves 4

Preheat the oven to 180°C (350°F/Gas 4). Using a sharp knife, cut the tops from 4 large red capsicums (peppers), then remove the seeds and membranes. Stand the capsicums in a small baking dish just large enough to fit them snugly. Drain and rinse a 400 g (14 oz) tin of chickpeas and place in a large bowl. Add the reserved pilaff, 75 g (2½ oz/ ½ cup) crumbled feta cheese and 1 large handful chopped parsley and mix well. Spoon the mixture into the capsicums and bake for 30 minutes, or until the capsicums are tender. Put 100 g (3½ oz) baby rocket (arugula) in a bowl and dress with 60 ml (2 fl oz/¼ cup) olive oil, 1 tablespoon lemon juice and 2 tablespoons finely chopped coriander (cilantro). Serve with the capsicums.

INDEX

In this index, all the main recipes in the book are listed without an asterisk. The 'leftover' recipes that are based on them and that appear in the colour side panels throughout this book are marked with an asterisk (*). To make these 'leftover' recipes, you will first need to prepare the main base recipe that appears with it on the same page, as the base recipe provides an important component for the leftover recipe.

Published in 2010 by Murdoch Books Pty Limited

Murdoch Books Australia
Pier 8/9
23 Hickson Road
Millers Point NSW 2000
Phone: +61 (0) 2 8220 2000
Fax: +61 (0) 2 8220 2558
www.murdochbooks.com.au

Murdoch Books UK Limited
Erico House, 6th Floor
93–99 Upper Richmond Road
Putney, London SW15 2TG
Phone: +44 (0) 20 8785 5995
Fax: +44 (0) 20 8785 5985
www.murdochbooks.co.uk

Publishing director: Kay Scarlett
Project editor: Kristin Buesing
Copy editor: Katri Hilden
Food editor: Leanne Kitchen
Cover concept: Yolande Gray
Design concept: Emilia Toia
Photographer: Stuart Scott
Stylist: Sarah O'Brien
Food preparation: Tina Asher, Kristin Buesing, Peta Dent
Recipes developed by: Nick Banbury, Peta Dent, Heidi Flett, Fiona Hammond, Vicky Harris, Leanne Kitchen, Kirrily La Rosa, Kim Meredith, Angela Tregonning and the Murdoch Books test kitchen
Production: Joan Beal

National Library of Australia Cataloguing-in-Publication Data
Title: My kitchen : love the leftovers : make two meals from one
ISBN: 978-1-74196-445-5 (hbk.)
Series: My kitchen series.
Notes: Includes index.
Subjects: Cookery (Leftovers)
Dewey Number: 641.552

A catalogue record for this book is available from the British Library.

PRINTED IN CHINA.

IMPORTANT: Those who might be at risk from the effects of salmonella poisoning (the elderly, pregnant women, young children and those suffering from immune deficiency diseases) should consult their doctor with any concerns about eating raw eggs.

OVEN GUIDE: You may find cooking times vary depending on the oven you are using. For fan-forced ovens, as a general rule, set the oven temperature to 20°C (35°F) lower than indicated in the recipe.

The **My Kitchen** series is packed with sensational flavours, simple methods and vibrant photographs. What's more, these easy, inexpensive and well-tested recipes use only commonly available ingredients and seasonal fresh produce. And because cooking should be a joy, there's a little bit of magic in these recipes too, in the form of smart short cuts and clever substitutions.

Love the Leftovers will save you time, energy and fussing in the kitchen. Why cook a meal from scratch every night when you can simply transform leftovers from one delicious dinner into a glorious new lunch or dinner the next day? Two different dishes from one. Summer or winter, the winner is you — twice over!

ISBN 978-1741964455

9 781741 964455

MURDOCH BOOKS